JOHN DONNE: THE ANNIVERSARIES

Twice or thrice had I loved thee,
Before I knew thy face or name;
So in a voice, so in a shapelesse flame . . .

—John Donne

JOHN DONNE: THE ANNIVERSARIES

EDITED WITH INTRODUCTION
AND COMMENTARY

BY

Frank Manley

THE JOHNS HOPKINS PRESS
BALTIMORE
1963

THIS BOOK HAS BEEN BROUGHT TO PUBLICATION WITH THE ASSISTANCE
OF A GRANT FROM THE FORD FOUNDATION.

for my mother and my father

Preface

The *Anniversaries* are Donne's most sustained effort: his longest poem and probably his greatest work, the product of his disturbed middle years and anguished maturity. The purpose of this edition is partly to establish the text of the poems, but primarily to make accessible, perhaps for the first time, the essential poetic act the text contains. To that end I have utilized all the means available to the literary critic—textual, critical, historical. If it succeeds, it is primarily because of the help and encouragement I have received from others.

My first and greatest debt is to my parents, who saw to it that I received an education at considerable hardship to themselves. It is to them that this volume is dedicated. Next, to my teachers, John E. Tilford, Jr., Charles R. Hart, Earl R. Wasserman, and Don Cameron Allen, who taught me in their various ways how to read. And finally to my wife, Carolyn, who knows with what patience she endured.

I was assisted financially by a number of grants from The Johns Hopkins University while I was a student there, particularly the Allen Dickey Fellowship. Most of the actual work on the edition was completed while on a fellowship of the Samuel S. Fels Foundation, which freed me from all other duties for the year and for which I am particularly grateful. The Fluid Research Fund of Yale University assisted in the final typing of the manuscript, and it is through the generosity of the Ford Foundation that it has been finally brought to publication.

Various libraries placed their resources at my disposal: The Johns Hopkins University Library and the library of the Tudor–Stuart Club, Yale University, Harvard University, The Henry E. Huntington Library, The Bodleian. I am particularly indebted to The Folger Shakespeare Library, where most of the initial collation was done. In addition, Sir Geoffrey L. Keynes graciously supplied me with photographic reproductions of the 1611 and 1612 editions in his personal possession, and Don Cameron Allen not only suggested books to me, but lent them as well from his own impressive collection of Renaissance Latin.

I am indebted to various readers: to Don Cameron Allen and Earl R. Wasserman, who read the manuscript in its first form as a dissertation; to Helen Gardner; to Louis L. Martz, particularly for his criticism of an early draft of the Introduction; and to Mrs. Nancy Gallienne of The Johns Hopkins University Press, who struggled with the notes. The greatest debt is to Don Cameron Allen. It was he who first suggested the subject, and it was his patience and kindness that saw it through to completion. He will know what I thank him for. But he will not know the more considerable debt that I share with all his students: the direct contact through him with the great tradition of Renaissance erudition and the lasting impression that to be a scholar is to be first of all a man.

Timothy Dwight College   FRANK MANLEY
Yale University

Contents

JOHN DONNE: THE ANNIVERSARIES

Introduction

I

ELIZABETH DRURY DIED in early December, 1610, two months before her fifteenth birthday. The churchwarden's accounts of St. Clement Danes, London, give simply and graphically all the known details:

> for the funerall of Sir Robart druryes daughter
> for the knell .... v^s
> for the Cloth .... ij^s vj^d
> for the passing bell .... iiij^d [1]

She was buried on December 17 in the chancel of the church of All Saints at Hawstead, Suffolk. Other than that almost nothing is known of her except a few legends. According to one she was killed by her own father; according to another she was to have married the "incomparable" Prince Henry, who also died an untimely death; and according to still another she loved a groom and died of grief when her father had him murdered.[2] Donne himself knew almost nothing about her. "Nobody can imagine," he wrote in one of his letters, "that I who never saw her, could

---

[1] R. C. Bald, *Donne and the Drurys* (Cambridge, 1959), p. 68.

[2] John Cullum, *The History and Antiquities of Hawstead in the County of Suffolk* (London, 1784), pp. 145–46; Bald, *op. cit.*, p. 68. These two works are the primary source of information on Donne's relation with the Drurys, particularly Bald.

have any other purpose in that, than that when I had received
so very good testimony of her worthiness, and was gone down
to print verses, it became me to say, not what I was sure was just
truth, but the best that I could conceive." [3] She was for Donne,
as she was for the rustics who made up tragic legends of her
death, simply a blank counter: an image of his own imagination
to be filled with whatever it possessed. She became for him not a
fairy princess in a folk tale, but something vaguely related and
at the same time infinitely stranger and more powerful. As he
explained to Ben Jonson, she was "the Idea of a Woman and not
as she was." [4]

Her father, Sir Robert Drury, was an important landowner
and wealthy man.[5] He is remembered today primarily in the
name Drury Lane, where his town house was once located. From
his few extant letters he seems to have been a rash, obstinate man,
self-confident, careless of speech, and a strong supporter of Es-
sex. He apparently had no literary interests, and it is difficult to
believe that he and Donne were ever intimate.[6] He was a courtier
and a soldier. He traveled considerably, kept up his estates, and
died relatively young, in 1615. His wife, Anne, was the daughter
of Sir Nicholas Bacon, of Redgrave, Suffolk, and the niece of
Sir Francis Bacon, the most illustrious member of the family.
She was apparently a religious woman with a genuine and sincere piety, but like her husband very little is known of her.
Judging from externals, however, her life does not seem to have
been particularly happy. She was apparently never very close to
her husband; at one time they actually separated. Her first child,
Dorothy, died in 1597 at the age of four. According to her
epitaph, "She only dreamt she liv'd / And then she dyde." [7]
Elizabeth died thirteen years later, leaving her childless. Her hus-

[3] Edmund Gosse, *The Life and Letters of John Donne* (London, 1899), I, 306.
[4] *Conversations with William Drummond of Hawthornden* in *Works*, ed. C. H. Here-
ford and Percy Simpson (Oxford, 1925), I, 133.
[5] By no means one of the wealthiest in England, however, as Gosse had implied;
see Bald, *op. cit.*, p. 65.
[6] It is perhaps significant that after a year's travel together on the Continent,
Donne mentions Drury only once in his letters and then only to deny the rumor
that Drury attended mass in Paris (*Ibid.*, p. 157).
[7] *Ibid.*, p. 29.

band died shortly afterward, and she spent the rest of her life widowed and alone.

The death of Elizabeth was naturally a very great shock to her parents. Her father erected a costly and imposing monument to her memory in the church at Hawstead. "This is a very pleasing monument," Sir John Cullum noted, "of painted alabaster and well executed; only disgraced by an ugly death's head."[8] The Latin epitaph, on a tablet of black marble, is undoubtedly by Donne.[9] Her father also established various charities in her honor. He founded six almshouses for poor, unmarried women in the villages on his estate and donated twenty-two pounds a year to the poor, signing his name to the document in letters of gold.[10] He also commissioned or in some way saw to it that her death was celebrated in two of the finest elegies in the language.

The circumstances surrounding the composition of the *Anniversaries* are not entirely known. It is not even known how Donne became acquainted with the Drurys. Recently R. C. Bald uncovered the previously unknown information that Donne's sister, Anne, married for the second time around 1593 a close friend of Sir Robert Drury's and that she actually lived in the Drury household from 1598 to 1603. That certainly would have given Donne an opportunity to meet the Drurys. But Anne's husband died in 1603, long before the *Anniversaries* were written, and there is no evidence that she continued the relationship with the Drurys afterward.[11] Another possibility is that Donne and Sir Robert Drury became acquainted at Cambridge. If Walton's account of Donne's education is correct, their stay would have overlapped by at least one year. But again there is no definite evidence one way or another. They both had many friends in common, however—Sir Henry Wotton, Sir Henry Goodyere, various acquaintances at Court—and it is entirely possible that one of them put them in touch with one another. Drury was in need of a poet, Donne of a patron.

---

[8] *Ibid.*, p. 53. There is a photograph in Bald, opposite p. 69.

[9] Reprinted in Cullum, *op. cit.*, pp. 53–54, and John Sparrow, "Two Epitaphs by John Donne," *TLS*, 26 March, 1949, p. 208.

[10] Cullum, *op. cit.*, pp. 75–76.

[11] Bald, *op. cit.*, pp. 69–84.

There is a fairly well-established tradition, apparently begun by E. K. Chambers in his edition of the poems in 1896, that Donne first wrote the short poem entitled *A Funerall Elegie* and when that seemed successful gradually enlarged it to two *Anniversaries*. But there is no real evidence that that was the case.[12] All that is known for certain is that *The First Anniversary* and the *Funerall Elegie* were printed together sometime in 1611. The *Funerall Elegie* was located at the end of the volume, after *The First Anniversary*. Presumably that is the way Donne arranged it to be read, and it is the only way the poem makes sense: it is dependent upon the symbolic process of *The First Anniversary* for its meaning.

Precisely when in 1611 the volume was published is not known; it was not entered on the Stationers' Register. It was remarkably well printed, with the body of the text in handsome italics. There are very few typographical errors, and it is pleasant to believe that Donne himself read proof since he was fastidious about such matters. But again nothing definite is known. The poems must have been successful with the Drurys, however, for they invited Donne to accompany them on their tour of the Continent in 1611–1612. The party left England in November, 1611. *The Second Anniversary* was probably begun at Amiens in December, 1611, on the first anniversary of Elizabeth's death, and it was completed in France as the allusion at the end of the poem (lines 511–18) makes clear. It was immediately sent to London; Joseph Hall wrote the *Harbinger;* and both poems were published, along with a reprint of *The First Anniversary*, by early April, 1612. The volume was rather badly printed, and when Donne returned to England in September, he drew up an

[12] The only external evidence is offered by Herbert Grierson, and it is incorrect. According to Grierson the *Praise of the Dead* and the *Anatomy of the World* were printed in italics in 1611 and the *Funerall Elegie* in ordinary roman type because Donne regarded the *Anatomy* as "introductory and subordinate to the *Elegie*," which had been written first. Later, when *The Second Anniversary* was added, the *Funerall Elegie* fell back into a subordinate position (*The Poems of John Donne* [Oxford, 1912], II, 178). The only difficulty is that Grierson's basic information is incorrect. In the 1611 edition the *Anatomy* was printed in italics and both the *Praise of the Dead* and the *Funerall Elegie* in roman. Both were thus distinguished from the main body of the text, the *Anatomy*.

errata slip, correcting some twenty-eight errors. Only one copy of the errata slip survived, presumably because most of the volumes had already been sold.

Other than that we know only that Donne wrote the poems at least in part as a business venture. In 1610 he was still casting about for a profession in a rather desperate struggle that had been going on for a number of years. He had just published *Pseudo-Martyr*, and for a brief time he apparently thought of making his living in some fashion by writing. It is from this period that most of the works published in his lifetime appear: *Pseudo-Martyr* (1610), *Ignatius his Conclave* (1611), commendatory verses for *Coryats Crudities* (1611), the *Elegie* on the death of Prince Henry in Sylvester's *Lachrymae Lachrymarum* (1613), and finally the *Anniversaries* (1611–1612). The reception of the *Anniversaries* apparently cured him of any such notions, however. He regretted publishing them almost as soon as they appeared and felt ashamed and humiliated at having degraded himself by becoming a professional poet:

> the fault that I acknowledge in myself is to have descended to print anything in verse, which, though it have excuse, even in our times, by example of men, which one would think should as little have done it, as I; yet I confess I wonder how I declined to it, and do not pardon myself.[13]

The difficulty over motive has proved one of the most serious obstacles to a proper understanding of the *Anniversaries*. Despite what we know today of the conventions of occasional verse in the Renaissance, the poems are still regarded with deep suspicion. But there is no real reason for it. Donne was naturally drawn closer to the Drurys as a result of the *Anniversaries*, but he was never a servile dependent flattering the memory of his patron's daughter to secure a roof over his head, as is often believed. Walton reported that Sir Robert Drury "assigned . . . [Donne] and his wife an useful apartment in his own large house at Drury Lane, and not only rent free, but was also a cherisher of

---

[13] Gosse, *op. cit.*, I, 302.

his studies, and such a friend as sympathized with him and his, in all their joy and sorrows." [14] R. C. Bald, however, has recently shown that Donne lived independently in a separate establishment on the property, in a "bricke howse . . . with a little passage and a smale Court to the same belonginge," which he occupied until he moved to the Deanery of St. Paul's in 1621. The Drurys helped somewhat with the furnishings. An inventory taken at Sir Robert's death records:

At Doctor Dunns

Item one Stammell furniture for a bedd with gold buttons and Copper lace	iij^{li}
Item one fether bedd one boulster twoe blancketts a Coveringe and twoe ould Redd Chayres	iij^{li}

But the house was not rent free. Donne apparently leased it since he is described as its tenant, not occupant, in all the surviving records. The amount of rent paid is not known. It may have been merely nominal. But the available evidence indicates that it was probably the full amount, sixteen pounds a year.[15]

That mitigates some of the suspicions surrounding the poems. But the fact remains that they were occasional poems written to order, in terms of the elegiac conventions of the day. They were designed to praise Elizabeth Drury as fulsomely as possible and at the same time assuage the grief of her family by externalizing it in the formal structure of the verse. But at the same time they were considerably more than that. Donne transformed the external occasion into something deeply personal; and it is ironic that it is precisely that symbolic level, mistaken as hyperbolic praise for Elizabeth Drury, that has made the poems seem so distasteful.

The *Anniversaries* were never very popular. As early as April, 1612, Donne received letters from England criticizing them in the same way they have been criticized ever since: that they say

---

[14] *Life of Donne*, cited by Bald, *op. cit.*, p. 113.
[15] *Ibid.*, pp. 113–17; 137.

too much, that the praise is too fulsome, the imagery too extravagant. Ben Jonson summed it up in his classic remark to William
Drummond of Hawthornden: "that Dones Anniversarie was
profane and full of Blasphemies/that he told Mr Donne, if it
had been written of ye Virgin Marie it had been something. . . ." Yet Donne always defended the poems. He replied
to the criticism in his letters:

> I hear from England of many censures of my book of Mistress
> Drury; if any of those censures do but pardon me my descent in print-
> ing anything in verse (which if they do they are more charitable
> than myself . . .), I doubt not but they will soon give over that
> other part of that indictment, which is that I have said so much;
> for nobody can imagine that I who never saw her, could have any
> other purpose in that, than that when I had received so very good
> testimony of her worthiness, and was gone down to print verses,
> it became me to say, not what I was sure was just truth, but the
> best that I could conceive; for that had been a new weakness in me,
> to have praised anybody in printed verses, that had not been capable
> of the best praise that I could give.[16]

And he told Jonson, in what is undoubtedly the most acute de-
fense of the poems ever made, "that he described the Idea of a
Woman and not as she was." The purpose of this introduction
will be in great part to expand the implications of that statement.

Later in the century the *Anniversaries* were imitated a number of times, though none of the imitations implies a very pro-
found criticism of the poems. Almost immediately after they
were written, they were used by Webster in his *Duchess of
Malfi* (1613), to help build up the context of allusion, the air
of mystery and sanctity surrounding his central character.[17]
William Drummond of Hawthornden imitated a number of
passages of *The First Anniversary*, particularly the new philosophy section, in his prose meditation on death, *The Cypresse*

---

[16] Gosse, *op. cit.*, I, 305–6.
[17] Most of the allusions are pointed out by Charles Crawford, *Collectanea*
(Stratford-on-Avon, 1907), I, 50–65.

Grove (1623). And some years later, in 1692, John Dryden celebrated the death of the Countess of Abdingdon in a "pane-gyrical" elegy entitled *Eleonora,* written directly in imitation of Donne's "admirable *Anniversaries."* Dryden never saw the Coun-tess of Abdingdon and therefore took the *Anniversaries* as the solution to the problem of how to write an elegy about someone of whom he knew nothing. In his hands, however, Donne's "Idea of a Woman" lost all its numen and became reduced to a flat, abstract pattern of virtue. As Dryden explained in the Preface to the poem:

> I have followed his [Donne's] footsteps in the design of his pane-gyric, which was to raise an emulation in the living, to copy out the example of the dead. And therefore it was that I once intended to have called this poem 'The Pattern;' and though, on a second con-sideration, I changed the title to the name of that illustrious person, yet the design continues, and Eleonora is still the pattern of charity, devotion, and humility; of the best wife, the best mother, and the best of friends.[18]

In the eighteenth century the *Anniversaries* were largely for-gotten, along with the rest of Donne. They were remembered, if at all, primarily through an allusion in *Spectator Paper, No. 41,* which quoted a few lines and remarked that they referred to one of Donne's mistresses. The error echoed through the cen-tury. Fielding, for example, picked it up in *Tom Jones* (IV, ii), where he has the same lines refer to Tom's mistress, Sophia. By the nineteenth century even the mistake in the *Spectator Papers* was forgotten.

In the twentieth century, however, the *Anniversaries* shared in the general rehabilitation of Donne, though they were not read as enthusiastically or as carefully as the *Songs and Sonets* or the *Divine Poems.* The general feeling was that despite a num-ber of passages as brilliant and complex as Donne ever wrote, the poems as a whole left one curiously unsatisfied and confused. Fifteen years ago, however, Louis L. Martz discovered that "the

[18] *Works,* ed. Sir Walter Scott, rev. George Saintsbury (Edinburgh, 1885), XI, 124.

full meaning of each [of the *Anniversaries*] grows out of a deliberately articulated structure" and that the structure is not essentially elegiac, but meditative, based on the strict principles of meditation established by Ignatius Loyola.[19] The discovery was extremely important. It established the process by which Donne transforms the death of Elizabeth Drury into an image of his own heart's loss of wisdom. But Martz failed to do anything with it. He regarded the poems as only partially successful. In *The Second Anniversary*, according to Martz, the meditative structure is organic; in *The First*, it is mechanical. One poem therefore is a success, the other a qualified failure.

The second major contribution to the study of the *Anniversaries* in this century was made by Marjorie Nicolson, who discovered that the poems are not two, but one: the antithetical poles of the same logical unit:

> The *Anniversaries* are . . . as artfully though not so obviously articulated as 'L'Allegro' and 'Il Penseroso.' The first is a lament over the body—the body of man and the body of the world—a meditation upon death and mortality. The second is a vision of the release of the soul from its prison. The whole, with antitheses of doubt and faith, despair and hope, death and the triumph of immortality, is a great symphony in which the harmony is more profound because of cacophony.[20]

The discovery was vitiated somewhat by Miss Nicolson's fantastic theory of the "Double Shee," but even there she was correct in recognizing some obscure symbolic process at work in the poems.

As a result of the work of Martz and Nicolson the *Anniversaries* have come to be regarded with something like respect, though no one purports to know precisely what they are about. Everyone agrees that they are meditations, that they have something to do with religion, and that they are in some way a

---

[19] "John Donne in Meditation: *The Anniversaries*," *ELH*, XIV (1947), 247–73, reprinted in *The Poetry of Meditation* (New Haven, 1954), pp. 219–48.
[20] *The Breaking of the Circle* (Evanston, Ill., 1950), pp. 65–66.

bridge between Donne's early and late verse, his love poetry and the *Divine Poems*. But other than that the criticism remains the same as it was in the seventeenth century: that the *Anniversaries* are "profane and full of Blasphemies." And the answer remains the same too, if we could once discover what it means: that they are about "the Idea of a Woman and not as she was."

II

The main problem with the *Anniversaries* is that they are unable to support the weight of their own hyperbole. They collapse under their own exaggerated burden of praise. According to most critics, they were obviously designed to lament the death of an idealized Elizabeth Drury. *The Second Anniversary* does that by and large, and for that reason it is generally regarded as the more successful of the two, in fact, "one of the great religious poems of the seventeenth century." [21] But *The First Anniversary* is usually considered a failure, "successful only in brilliant patches," full of "pseudo-scientific paraphernalia," "ponderous redundancy," and "splendid fustian." [22] It too, apparently, was designed to present a portrait of Elizabeth Drury in the Petrarchan fashion as an idealized form, a lost pattern of virtue. But instead, the central emotion of the poem, the overwhelming sense of loss, is ultimately not connected with the death of Elizabeth Drury. It is a lament for the loss of Eden, though the two are strangely and disconcertingly confused. According to Louis L. Martz, there is

> a central inconsistency [in the poem] which defeats all Donne's efforts to bring its diverse materials under control. For it is not correct to say, as Empson says, that 'the complete decay of the universe' is presented as having been caused by the death of Elizabeth Drury. If this were so, the poem might achieve unity through supporting a dominant symbol of virtue's power, and one might be able

[21] Martz, *Poetry of Meditation*, p. 221.
[22] Mario Praz, *The Flaming Heart* (New York, 1958), pp. 200–1.

to agree with Empson that the 'only way to make the poem sensible is to accept Elizabeth Drury as the Logos.' But, after the Introduction has elaborately presented this hyperbole, one discovers in the first Meditation that Elizabeth Drury has, basically, nothing to do with the sense of decay in the poem.[23]

Donne takes a series of traditional meditations on the decay of the world from its beginning in Eden to its final putrefaction in the present, juxtaposes them with a series of fulsome, exaggerated eulogies of Elizabeth Drury, and argues that they are one and the same thing. The trouble is obviously the causality involved. It is difficult to consider the death of Elizabeth Drury as equivalent to the fall of man, and all Donne's efforts to force the two together results only in exaggerating their difference and increasing the sense of hyperbole. "The imagery seems extravagant—even blasphemous—not because of what we know about the circumstances of the poem's composition, but because the imagery is not supported by the poem as a whole." [24] As Ben Jonson remarked, "if it had been written of ye Virgin Marie it had been something."

Mario Praz, for example, compares the poems with Donne's lyric, "A Feaver," which he believes is in the same tradition and elaborates fundamentally the same conceit.[25] A girl is dying, and Donne argues that her fever is the fire destined to consume the world. If she were to die, the whole world would vapor with her breath.

> Or if, when thou, the worlds soule, goest,
>   It stay, tis but thy carkasse then,
> The fairest woman, but thy ghost,
>   But corrupt wormes, the worthyest men.
>
> [9–12]

Praz implies that the lyric is successful partly because of its passionate, dramatic brevity—it is not stretched out for over a

---

[23] Martz, op. cit., p. 229.
[24] Ibid., p. 233.
[25] Praz, op. cit., pp. 199–201.

thousand lines—but also because its emotions are felt to be valid. Donne is speaking of the feeling, often caused by the death of a loved one, that the world has lost its meaning and therefore its substantiality:

> Conceive yourself, if possible, suddenly stripped of all the emotion with which your world now inspires you, and try to imagine it *as it exists,* purely by itself, without your favorable or unfavorable, hopeful or apprehensive comment. It will be almost impossible for you to realize such a condition of negativity and deadness. No one portion of the universe would then have importance beyond another; and the whole collection of its things and series of its events would be without significance, character, expression, or perspective.[26]

It is the same as a person's saying he has nothing left to live for. What he means is that there is nothing in the world that makes it alive for him. Everything has receded into the cold, impersonal sameness that it is in essence.

The *Anniversaries,* on the other hand, do not seem sincere. Elizabeth Drury was nothing to Donne; the whole world could not have vapored away for him with her breath. He failed to make the emotion convincing because his heart was not in it, and the poems are therefore a failure.

Ultimately, I think, Martz and Praz are wrong. The problem of sincerity in literature is extremely complex. The *Anniversaries* are not lyrics and should not be judged as though they were. It is quite possible for Donne to have realized the absurdity of the world through the death of Elizabeth Drury without being touched by any deep, personal grief. In fact, I think that is precisely what happened. In the *Anniversaries* Donne is speaking of the same sickness of the spirit as in "A Feaver," but not in terms of Petrarchan tradition and not in terms of the girl herself. It is not caused by any personal grief, but by something deeper and more intense.

Yet even in terms of their own argument, Martz and Praz are not entirely correct. Granted there is no literal relation be-

[26] William James, *The Varieties of Religious Experience* (New York, 1902), p. 150.

tween the death of Elizabeth Drury and the decay of the world, the juxtaposition still makes sense of sorts. The image of woman in the poem, the idealized Elizabeth Drury, remains recognizably Elizabeth Drury, but through the process of the poem, she also becomes something much more—partly through the prevalent Platonism of the day, the cult and worship of the lady as the representative of spiritual things: beauty of the soul, outer and inner harmony—and partly through the more universal tendency to regard woman in general as an image of Eden summarizing in herself the land of the heart's desire. Donne himself never claimed a literal identity; even in the title he asks only that we see the frailty and decay of this whole world *represented* in the untimely death of Elizabeth Drury. And as Marjorie Nicolson has pointed out, he never spoke of her as anything other than a mysterious "Shee." It is up to us in other words to allow the poem to make sense, not literally, any more than the conceit behind "A Feaver" makes sense in any literal way, but in a poetic, metaphoric way.

Moreover, the readers of Donne's time would have seen an appropriateness we do not in his linking together, even as violently as he does, the death of this girl with the effects of original sin. For it was well known that sin brought death into the world, and all our woe. "By one man sin entered into the world, and death by sin; and so death passed upon all men, for that all have sinned: . . . death reigned from Adam to Moses, even over them that had not sinned after the similitude of Adam's transgression, who is the figure of him that was to come." [27] Here is an example of death, Donne says in effect, which can be used to explain and understand the cause of all death. This girl died young, and so did the world, or what was best in it. The rest has been merely a process of living putrefaction. Donne has taken, in other words, a particular example of mortality and in meditating on it universalized it and found in it the source of all mortality, not only the sum total of all things that ever were or ever will be in this world, but the whole frame and fabric of the universe itself. The mysterious "Shee" in the poem

[27] Romans 5:12, 14.

is in a sense Elizabeth Drury, but she is also a symbolic creature: the idealized form in Donne's own mind of a perfect pattern of virtue. She is the "Idea of a Woman," a symbol of all the beauty man and the universe lost in the fall: the order and harmony of the outer world as well as the inner beauty of virtue we ourselves, each individual, have lost. She is the only thing this last, dying age of the world had left, the only memory of the old times in Eden. And at the same time she is the image of its mortality and evanescence.

Beyond that, however, is something else. Marjorie Nicolson referred to it in a footnote to her theory of the "Double Shee":

> As I leave this particular problem of identification and interpretation, I make an *apologia* of my own. I do not pretend to have solved all Donne's riddles—if riddles they were—in the *Anniversary Poems*. . . . While I am persuaded that the three chief women in 'Shee' are the Virgin Mary, Astraea, and particularly [Queen] Elizabeth, I suspect that there is at least one other 'She' and 'Shee' I cannot yet identify. Some passages, particularly toward the beginning of the *Second Anniversary*, lead me to think that Donne was including among his 'Virgins' a woman recently dead, who was not Elizabeth Drury.[28]

William Empson and Charles Coffin recognized the same difficulty: "The only way to make the poem sensible is to accept Elizabeth Drury as the Logos." [29] "This is the heavy burden of religion and philosophy shouldered upon the fragile story of the life and death of Elizabeth Drury. Unless we recognize in her brief encounter with human experience the lofty parallel to the incarnation of Christ himself, Donne's attempt is hopeless. . . . Though Christ is not named in either of the *Anniversaries*, He is definitely figured forth as Elizabeth Drury." [30]

Critics have constantly felt that there is something more to the poems than mere Petrarchanism, something that they were not

---

[28] Nicolson, *op. cit.*, p. 88*n*.

[29] William Empson, *English Pastoral Poetry* (New York, 1938), p. 84.

[30] Charles M. Coffin, *John Donne and the New Philosophy* (New York, 1938), pp. 276, 258.

quite able to put their finger on. Either the poems are a failure, or what seems to be fantastic hyperbole is in fact a burden of extra symbolic meaning that must be understood before the poems begin to make sense. The only trouble is that symbolism of that sort seems to be out of the question. For by asking us to consider Elizabeth Drury as an Eden-image of vague and unnamed desire, Donne begins a process of coalescence that ends by making her not the sign of Eden and therefore separate from it, but in some literal way the thing itself. Through the poetry, the fundamental poetic act, what emerges is a mythical figure of woman on whom literally the entire world depends. And yet that woman remains Elizabeth Drury. It is not logical, it does not make sense, and at this point most criticism breaks down.

But perhaps the difficulty is with us and not with the poem. For true symbols are almost always illogical. They represent a state of mind and a way of understanding prior to logic, and that is what supposedly distinguishes them from signs. Both signs and symbols point to something beyond themselves, but "while the sign bears no necessary relation to that to which it points, the symbol participates in the reality of that for which it stands." [31] Signs exist only to have the veil of their meaning swept away, whereas symbols do not proceed beyond themselves; they are unable to be translated into other terms and by that very fact open up "a level of reality for which non-symbolic speaking is inadequate." [32] As Dante pointed out in his *Letter to Can Grande,*

> we see many things through the intellect for which words (*signa vocalia*) are lacking and which Plato managed to imply (*insinuat*) in his books by assuming metaphors for them (*per assumptionem metaphorismorum*): for he saw many things through the intellectual light which he was not able to express in ordinary speech.[33]

More precisely, it is similar to the distinction in the *Convivio* between the allegory of poets and the allegory of theologians.

[31] Paul Tillich, *Systematic Theology* (Chicago, 1951), I, 239.
[32] Paul Tillich, *Theology of Culture,* ed. R. C. Kimball (New York, 1959), p. 56.
[33] *Tutte le Opere,* ed. E. Moore (Oxford, 1897), p. 420.

One is fictive: "a truth hidden under the beautiful lie." [34] But the other is real:

> The author of Holy Scripture is God, in whose power it is to signify his meaning not only by words, which man also can do, but also by things themselves. And so, whereas in all sciences words signify things, this science [theology] has this property, that the things signified by words also signify something. Therefore the first meaning, in which words signify things, pertains to the first sense, which is the historical or literal sense. That meaning in which the things signified by words, again signify other things is called the spiritual sense, which is based on the literal and presupposes it. [35]

Religious symbols in particular "are directed towards the infinite which they symbolize *and* toward the finite through which they symbolize it. They force the infinite down to finitude and the finite up to infinity. They open the divine for the human and the human for the divine." [36] According to this distinction, for example, Petrarch's Laura would be a sign; Beatrice and Elizabeth Drury, symbols.

But the problem then becomes, what is she a symbol of? And the answer is not easy, any easier than it is with Beatrice. The general area seems clear enough. She has to do with the state of our own souls. As Donne explains in the very first lines of the poem:

> When that rich soule which to her Heauen is gone,
> Whom all they celebrate, who know they haue one,
> (For who is sure he hath a soule, vnlesse
> It see, and Iudge, and follow worthinesse,

[34] *Convivio*, II, i, 2–4, cited in Charles S. Singleton, *Dante Studies* 1: *Commedia, Elements of Style* (Cambridge, Mass., 1954), p. 85. For the distinction between the two types of allegory, see the entire chapter, pp. 84–98. For a similar concept, in Donne's own time, see Bacon's distinction between ciphers and hieroglyphics in *De Augmentis*, VI, 1.

[35] Aquinas, *Summa*, I, Q. 1, a. 10, cited in Singleton, p. 88. I have altered the translation slightly.

[36] Tillich, *Systematic Theology*, I, 240.

And by Deedes praise it? He who doth not this,
May lodge an In-mate soule, but tis not his.)   [1–6]

She is not only directly identified as a "rich soule" herself, but
she is celebrated only by those who know they have a soul; and
celebrated in this sense means not only *memorialized* but also
reinacted, reperformed, as in the celebration of the mass. As
Donne explains a little later on (lines 67–78), "the matter and
the stuffe" of the new world created in her memory is her virtue,
but "the forme our practise is." She has to do with the *possi-
bilitatem boni* Augustine thought was lost in the fall, the innate
uprightness of the soul which is restored only by grace.[37] She
is the soul's likeness to God, the "intrinsique balme" that pre-
serves it from the putrefaction of spiritual death:

Physitians say, That man hath in his Constitution, in his Complexion,
a naturall vertue, which they call *Balsamum suum*, his owne Balsamum, by which, any wound which a man could receive in his body,
would cure it selfe, if it could be kept cleane from the anoiances of
the aire, and all extrinsique encumbrances. Something that hath some
proportion and analogy to this Balsamum of the body, there is in
the soule of man too. The soule hath *Nardum suam*, her Spikenard
. . . , a naturall disposition to Morall goodnesse, as the body hath
to health. But therein lyes the souls disadvantage, that whereas the
causes that hinder the cure of a bodily wound, are extrinsique offences
of the Ayre, and putrefaction from thence, the causes in the wounds
of the soule, are intrinsique, so as no other man can apply physick
to them; Nay, they are hereditary, and there was no time early inough
for our selves to apply any thing by way of prevention, for the
wounds were as soone as we were, and sooner.[88]

[37] Cf. Donne, *Sermons*, ed. George R. Potter and Evelyn M. Simpson (Berkeley and
Los Angeles, 1953–62), II, 55: "in that wound, as wee were all shot in *Adam*,
we bled out *Impassibilitatem*, and we sucked in *Impossibilitatem*; There we lost our
Immortality, our *Impassibility*, our assurance of Paradise, and then we lost *Possibilita-
tem boni*, says S. *Augustine*: all possibility of recovering any of this by our selves."
Hereafter cited as *Sermons*.
[88] *Sermons*, V, 347–49.

But all that remains metaphoric and vague. There is no clear, explicit identification of the symbolism in the poem, and for that reason it has run off in the minds of critics to Jesus Christ or the Catholic Church, Queen Elizabeth, the Virgin Mary, the Logos, Astraea. There is nothing to bring it into sharp focus, and we are left with a feeling of incompleteness.

I am not certain that any sharp focus is possible. The symbol is too complex for all its parts to be held in the mind at once discursively. Moreover, it is the nature of symbols to suggest more than they seem to contain. They resist all efforts at precise, intellectual definition. But in present-day terms perhaps a vague idea of what Donne was getting at is available in C. G. Jung's concept of the *anima,* which is in itself vague, but which in general represents the "Idea of a Woman" in man, the image of his own soul, his own deepest reality. It is a universal symbol of otherness in man, either of desire, the completion of one's own androgynous self, as in the Platonic myth, or of strange intuitive knowledge otherwise unavailable to him, "a source of information about things for which a man has no eyes." [39] In Donne's own time, however, the clearest formulation was in terms of the traditional concept of Wisdom, which, like the *anima,* was almost always symbolized by woman, who represented the subconscious, intuitive, feminine intelligence of the heart as opposed to the active, conscious, masculine intelligence of the mind. "What is Wisdome?" Donne asks, modifying the ancient Stoic definition:

> we may content our selves, with that old definition of Wisdome, that it is *Rerum humanarum, & divinarum scientia;* The Wisdome that accomplishes this cleannesse, is the knowledge, the right valuation of this world, and of the next; To be able to compare the joyes of heaven, and the pleasures of this world, and the gaine of the one, with the losse of the other, this is the way to this cleanenesse of the heart; because that heart that considers, and examines, what it takes in, will take in no foule, no infectious thing [*Sermons,* VII, 336].

[39] *The Collected Works of C. G. Jung,* ed. H. Read, M. Fordham, and G. Adler (New York, 1953), VII, 186.

It is that Wisdom that the total experience of the *Anniversaries* presents. Donne says in effect:

> Looke then upon the greatnes of God and the smalnesse of man; the goodnes of God, and the vilenesse of man; the wisdome of God, and the folly of man; the love of God, and the hate of man; the grace of God, and the disgrace of man; the mercy of God, and tyranny of man; and the glory of God, and the infamy of man: and fixing the eye of the heart upon the one and the other, how canst thou but to the glory of God, and shame of thy selfe . . . cry with the Prophet David, *Oh Lord what is man that thou doest visit him?* [40]

It forms the essential structure of each poem—the alternation of contempt for the world (meditation) and praise of virtue (eulogy)—as well as the total structure of both poems taken together as a unit. In the first Donne realizes imagistically, through the death of a girl he never saw, the grace and the indwelling wisdom of God, *sapientia creata,* that was lost in the fall; and the entire movement is downward to decay. In the second, however, he has found his direction; through the realization of his soul's loss he has regained the wisdom that orients him toward God, and the entire poem surges upward toward eternal life. It is as a concrete image of that Wisdom, its direct emotional apprehension, that the mysterious figure of woman at the center of the poem is best understood. She is in herself both the object and the wit: the realization as well as the means to realize it, for the only way to understand the *Anniversaries* is intuitively, through symbolic understanding. The poems make sense only to those who realize, with Donne, that

>   no thing
> Is worth our trauaile, griefe, or perishing,
> But those rich ioyes, which did possesse her hart,
> Of which shee's now partaker, and a part.
>   [*The First Anniversary,* 431–434]

---

[40] Nicholas Breton, *Divine Considerations of the Soule* (1608), cited in Martz, *op. cit.,* pp. 227–28.

According to Augustine, in a phrase echoed by Donne in the opening lines of the poem, they only know they have a soul who see (*meminit*), judge (*intelligit*) and follow (*diligit*) God; and "that is true wisdom": *quod est sapientia.*[41]

III

The tradition of Wisdom in the Renaissance is extremely complex. It is not one, but many, a loose cluster of traditions that were never completely unified, never fused or assimilated into one another. They were either superimposed upon one another by various syncretic mythographers or simply regarded as parallel forms, analogous discoveries of the same basic truth. It was vague and inchoate, more suggestive than precise, and what made it even vaguer and ultimately more mysterious was that it was never completely assimilated into Christianity except perhaps in abstract theological terms that made a botch of the symbolism and turned Christ allegorically into a woman. It was by and large inaccessible, beyond the limits of ordinary perception, but it was nevertheless there, latent, available to those who recognized in it something analogous to their own experience. In its extreme form it was either madness, as it was for Guillaume Postel, or it was madness translated into great poetry, as with Dante and Donne.[42] It was a symbolic realization of God's grace

---

[41] *De Trinitate, PL* 42, 1047.

[42] Postel's account of his experience with Mère Jehanne matches Dante's almost point for point, except that what Dante transformed into poetry, Postel revealed in all its essential madness. Sometime between 1547 and 1549, immediately after he was expelled from the Society of Jesus for heresy, Postel met a woman of fifty whom he referred to variously as the Venetian Virgin, the New Eve, or the *Mater Mundi*. She was able to see through solid objects and could call up visions of Satan bound in the center of the earth. Although she was illiterate, she was able to explain to him all the secrets of the *Zohar,* and he began to speak of her as "the most admirable of all creatures who have ever been, are, or will be," "the consummation of the mystery of eternity," a person "in whom dwells the fullness of the substance of Christ," "the image of her spouse our father who is in heaven."

In the summer of 1549 Postel prepared to leave Venice for a trip to the Near East. Mère Jehanne prophesied to him that she would die while he was gone, but that she and her husband Jesus would send him

and his indwelling, the light that filled Milton's blindness, visiting him nightly, and the beauty of Beatrice in Eden, on the summit of Mount Purgatory.

Generally speaking there were two main lines of tradition, one Greek, one Hebraic. The Greek began with Pausanias' account of Aphrodite Urania in Plato's *Symposium*. In Pausanias' terms it was simply a sign, a figure of speech representing the love of virtue and the practice of philosophy, as opposed to the

---

two beautiful gifts in our two garments, and you shall be our first born son, who shall cause to be understood by Intellect and Reason the truth of our mysteries. The two gifts will be, one the perfection of the Brain and Restored intelligence, and the other the consummation of the heart and true repaired Reason.

She died as she had said, but two years later she returned to him and literally took possession of him: "her spiritual body and substance sensibly descended into me and sensibly extended throughout my body." He described the experience fully in his *Prime nove del altro mondo,* published in 1555. Shortly after Christmas, 1551, his "most glorious Mother" appeared to him and presented him with the spiritual garments she had promised him earlier. As soon as he put them on, he felt himself immediately changed. His bones dissolved one by one; his flesh was penetrated by "thousands of Angelic virtues and operations." His entire physical substance was remade. He was literally reborn and from that time forward felt neither hunger nor thirst nor the need for sleep. Even the food he ate dissolved in air, so that "scarcely the hundreth part follows the natural course."

Postel was obviously insane, but the important thing is not the insanity, but the parallel with Dante and beyond that the essential similarity between Mère Jehanne and the Idea of a Woman in the *Anniversaries:*

I testify [Postel wrote] . . . to the whole church and to future generations of the human race, that I understand and wish to understand nothing else, when I speak of this middle nature, the *anima mundi,* whose highest cause is the *maternitas generalis,* just as the *paternitas generalis* stems from God, than the accumulation, heap, pile, combination, or congregation of divine virtues through which God, otherwise absolutely motionless and unmoving, acts on particular occasions; and through which He who has no position in space, filling everything without place of His Own, nevertheless in this heaping up of divine virtues becomes localized; I mean the Shekinah, or localized and moving providence, by means of which God disposes of all things, and rules and sustains in place, just as our soul, lacking a definite place and without motion of its own, nevertheless through its own virtues rules and sustains locally while dispersed throughout the whole body.

See William J. Bouwsma, *Concordia Mundi: The Career and Thought of Guillaume Postel* (1510–1581) (Cambridge, Mass., 1957), pp. 13–18, 146–64.

more earthly love of the flesh. But it was also loosely associated with the desire for things divine, imperfectly remembered, and ultimately with the abstract, intellectual beauty which the wise Diotoma told Socrates was located at the end of the soul's ascent, in the realm of eternal ideas: "beauty absolute, separate, simple, and everlasting, which without diminution and without increase, or any change, is imparted to the ever-growing and perishing beauties of all other things."

'This, my dear Socrates,' said the stranger of Mantineia, 'is that life above all others which man should live, in the contemplation of beauty absolute; a beauty which if you once beheld, you would see not to be after the measure of gold, and garments, and fair boys and youths, . . . [but] divine beauty . . . pure and clear and unalloyed, not clogged with the pollutions of mortality and all the colours and vanities of human life.' [43]

Among later Platonists the concept of the *Venus Coelestis* became much more important. It was no longer regarded half-doubtfully as a myth or a figure of speech, but was literally the thing itself, not a sign, but a symbol which participated directly in the reality of that for which it stood. According to Ficino she was the intelligence of the Angelic Mind, the incorporeal world that forms the first emanation of the cosmos, imperfect only inasmuch as it is created and exists by its participation in God. Impelled (*rapitur*) by the force of an innate love (*amore ingenito*) she contemplates eternally the beauty of God. She contains (*complectitur*) its splendor within herself, in its first perfection, and transmits it to lower forms, where it gleams with flashes of an unearthly light (*fulgoris illius scintillas*). She is the figure of perfect contemplation, the mind free from the trammels of corporeal existence, as it is in itself in the pure act of thought: "The first Venus, which is the mind, is said to have been born of the sky without a mother because *mother* (*mater*) is said by physicists to be related to *matter* (*materia*). All com-

[43] *The Dialogues of Plato*, trans. B. Jowett (New York and London, 1892), I, 381; 382.

merce with corporeal matter, however, is foreign to the mind." [44]
The idea is obviously related to the Christian concept of the
Logos or the Word, the second person of the Trinity, who contains the divine Ideas within himself and, as the source of creation, puts them into operation in the world—in whom was life,
"and the life was the light of men" (John 1:4). The Florentine
Neoplatonists undoubtedly felt the similarity. They spoke of
them in the same terms, using one to understand the other, but
they denied any literal identity. Pico, for example, in his commentary on Benivieni's *Canzone de Amore* identifies the Celestial Venus as the Logos or the Word, but is careful to indicate
that he is speaking of a Neoplatonic, not a Christian concept, a
sapientia creata that exists neither in God nor in man, but in a
realm of intermediate being:

[44] *Commentarium in Convivium Platonis, de Amore,* ed. Raymond Marcel (Paris,
1956), pp. 154–55. The Angelic Mind of the Florentine Neoplatonists corresponds
to Plotinus' νοῦς. In the Middle Ages Bernard Silvestris in his *De universitate mundi*
identified the Noys (νοῦς) as a female emanation of the deity, the "Intellect of the
highest God" and "Providence." She shares in the being of the godhead directly,
but at the same time is an intermediary between God and matter. Her daughter's
name is *Natura*. In heaven Noys sits enthroned between the Cherubim and Seraphim.
Some authors identified her with the world soul, but at the same time argued that
a Platonic identification of that sort was invalidated by Genesis (*PL* 189, 1515).
See E. R. Curtius, *European Literature and the Latin Middle Ages,* trans. W. R.
Trask (New York, 1953), pp. 108–13; 121–22.
   Silvestris identified the Celestial Venus with "the music of the spheres (*mundanum
musicam*), that is, the harmony (*aequalem proportionem*) of all things in the universe. Some call her *Astraea*, others *natural justice*. For she is to be found in the elements, in the stars, in the seasons (*temporibus*), in living things" (*Commentum
super sex libros Eneidos Vergili,* ed. W. Riedel, p. 9, cited in Richard H. Green,
"Alan of Lille's *De Planctu Naturae,*" *Speculum,* XXXI [1956], 668). According
to John Scotus Eriugena, she is "a figure of the *rationales seminales*, of Nature herself, and of the providential love by which the universe of created things is produced and reproduced." But she is also identified with the natural goodness and
virtue of the human soul (*bonas ac naturales humanae animae virtutes*) that were
lost in the fall (Green, p. 667).
   In the eighteenth century Pope spoke of Mother Dulness in *The Dunciad* (an inversion of the traditional image of Wisdom) as "a God without a Thought" (IV,
485): "Thine is the genuine head of many a house,/ And much Divinity, without
a Noûs" (IV, 243–44). Cf. also Clement of Alexandria, who, according to the
Dictionnaire de Théologie Catholique, believed that "La véritable image de Dieu,
c'est le Verbe divin, et l'image de cette image c'est le νοῦς humain" (*s.v., Péché
Originel*).

We therefore . . . affirm, That God from eternity produced a creature of incorporeal and intellectual nature, as perfect as is possible
for a created being, beyond which he produced nothing. . . . We
conclude . . . that no creature but this first minde proceeds immediately from God; for of all other effects issuing from this minde,
and all other second causes God is onely the mediate efficient. This
by Plato, Hermes and Zoroaster is called the Daughter of God,
Τέκνον τοῦ αγαθοῦ, νοῦς, σοφια, θεῖος λόγος, the *Minde*, *Wisdom*,
Divine Reason, by some interpreted *the Word*: not meaning (with
our Divines) the Son of God, he not being a creature, but one essence coequal with the Creator.[45]

She is also known as *Paradise*:

Nature in it self inform, when it receives form from God is the
Angelick Minde; this form is Ideas, the first Beauty; . . . the in-
digence of that inform nature we termed *Jupiter* (I. 8.) *in whose
Garden* the Ideas are planted, with these the first Minde adorned, was
by the Ancients named Paradise; to which contemplative life and
eternal felicity Zoroastres inviting us saith, *Seek, seek Paradise*: Our
Divines transfer it to the *Coelum Empyraeum*, the seat of the happy
Souls, whose blessedness consists in contemplation and perfection of
the Intellect, according to *Plato*.[46]

It is the theme of both *Anniversaries: Seek, seek Paradise.*

Since in the Platonic scheme of things the visible world is
simply an imperfect image of the invisible, the Celestial Venus

[45] *The Poems and Translations of Thomas Stanley*, ed. Galbraith M. Crump (Oxford, 1962), p. 199. Cf. Augustine, *Confessions*, XII, 15: "There is a certain sublime
creature that clings to the true and truly eternal God with so chaste a love that
although not coeternal with him, nevertheless is not separated from him and dissolved (*defluat*) into the variety and vicissitude of time, but rests (*requiescat*) in
the truest contemplation of him only. . . . For Wisdom was created before all
things—not that Wisdom which is clearly coeternal to you, our God, his Father,
the Wisdom through which all things were made and in the beginning of which
(*in quo principio*) you created heaven and earth—but Wisdom that is created: that
is, the intellectual nature, which by the contemplation of light, is light." Slightly
further on he identifies this creature as "the rational and intellectual mind of your
chaste city, our mother, who is above and is free (*libera*) and eternal in the heavens."
[46] Pico, *op. cit.*, p. 209. .

also has her counterpart in the mind of man. Ficino put it suc-
cinctly: *Mens nostra que prima in nobis Venus est:* "When the
mind, which is the Celestial Venus in man, first perceives the
outward beauty of the human body, it worships and desires it as
an image of the divine beauty, and oftentimes is transported
from one to the other." [47] At the first creation, Ficino explains,
following Plato's myth of androgynous man, the soul was
adorned with two lights (*luminibus*), one innate and the other
infused (*ingenito et infuso; naturale e sopranaturale*). The innate light was directed toward things equal and inferior, the
infused, toward things superior. When, through pride, the soul
attempted to become equal with God and turned inward upon
itself, utilizing only its own, innate light, it cut itself off from
contact with things above. It lost the infused light (*splendorem*)
of grace and immediately fell into matter. The implication is
that the light that was lost is precisely the same beauty the soul
perceives when it rises to wholeness once again:

> When the soul which is cut off and immersed in the body arrives at
> the age of adolescence, it is urged by a zeal for truth on the part of
> the natural, innate light it has still preserved to search out the in-
> fused divine light which was once the other half of itself and which
> it lost in falling. Once it has recovered it, the soul is complete again
> and finds its beatitude in the vision of God.[48]

Wisdom becomes a form of celestial love. If the soul proceeds
by degrees from the love of the human body upward from corporeal to incorporeal, at each stage rarefying its perception and
coming closer to absolute, intellectual beauty, it eventually
arrives at a vision of *la celeste Venere in propria forma:*

> turning into her self, shee [the soul] findes the Image of Ideal Beauty
> communicated to her by the Intellect, the Object of Celestial Love.

[47] Ficino, *op. cit.,* p. 155.
[48] *Ibid.,* p. 169. For an excellent commentary on the passage linking it to Genesis
on the one hand and the wild imaginings of Francis George on the other, see Marin
Mersenne, *Observationes et Emendationes ad Francisci Georgii Veneti Problemata*
(Lutetiae Parisiorum, 1623), cols. 43–44.

5. She ascends from this Idea in her self, to the place where Celestial *Venus* is, in her proper form: Who in fulness of her Beauty not being comprehensible, by any particular Intellect, she as much as in her lies, endeavours to be united to the first Minde, the chiefest of Creatures, and general Habitation of Ideal Beauty, obtaining this, she terminates, and fixeth her journey.[49]

At the deepest point within ourselves we perceive the Celestial Venus. She is mind, but she is not what we usually think of as mind. She appears only when the ordinary processes of the mind are put to sleep. She is more like the soul, but she is also something from beyond the self. She is God's "owne Beloved," according to Spenser, "The soveraine dearling of the Deity"—an image of universal, spiritual beauty divorced from things of sense:

> For in the view of her celestiall face
> All joy, all blisse, all happinesse have place,
> Ne ought on earth can want unto the wight
> Who of her selfe can win the wishfull sight.[50]

She is not an abstraction, but something deeper, beyond the reach of abstraction: a symbol of what is essentially a subrational inclination of the heart. Whoever is given the grace to perceive her is transported "from flesh into the spright":

> Ne from thenceforth doth any fleshly sense,
> Or idle thought of earthly things remaine;
> But all that earst seemd sweet seemes now offense,
> And all that pleased earst now seemes to paine:

---

[49] Pico, *op. cit.*, p. 228. For an extension as well as a popularization of the idea, see Christoforo Giarda's "Architectress and Inventrix of symbolical images" in his *Liberalium Disciplinarum Icones Symbolicae Bibliothecae Alexandrinae*, ed. Joannes Georgius Graevius (Lugduni Batavorum, 1723), IX, vi, 2.

[50] "An Hymme of Heavenly Beautie," lines 242–45. For excellent, if mutually contradictory commentaries on Spenser's Sapience, see J. B. Fletcher, "A Study in Renaissance Mysticism: Spenser's 'Fowre Hymnes'," *PMLA*, XXVI (1911), 452–75; C. G. Osgood, "Spenser's Sapience," *SP*, XIV (1917), 167–77; D. Saurat, "La 'Sapience' de Spenser et la Schekhina de la Cabale," *Revue de Littérature Comparée*, VI (1926), 5–15; Josephine W. Bennett, "The Theme of Spenser's *Fowre Hymnes*," *SP*, XXVII (1931), 18–57.

Their joy, their comfort, their desire, their gaine,
Is fixed all on that which now they see;
All other sights but fayned shadowes bee.

[267–273]

It was ultimately a form of ecstasy, in which the mind of man
actively participated in the wisdom of God:

> with this sight Moses saw, Paul saw, and many other of the elect
> saw the face of the Lord; and this is the sight our theologians call
> intellectual cognition, intuitive knowledge; with this sight, St. John
> the Evangelist says the just will see high God, and this is the whole
> of our reward.[51]

"Intellectual cognition, intuitive knowledge" in the traditional
definition was an infusion of grace, *de sursum descendens,* which
allowed the soul to perceive the beauty of God. According to
Aquinas, knowledge is possible only when the knower contains
in his own nature the thing that is to be known. "Therefore, the
created intellect is not able to perceive God through its own nature, except insofar as God joins himself to the created intellect
through grace and allows himself to become intelligible through
himself." [52] It corresponds to the infused light Ficino believed
was lost by the soul when it fell into matter:

> To know God, man, in his condition after the fall, needs a medium,
> which is like a mirror in which appears the image of God; for it is
> necessary that we arrive at the invisible things of him from the
> things that are made, according to *Romans,* I. In the state of in-
> nocence, however, man did not need this medium; but he did need a
> medium which is as it were a species of thing seen (*quasi species rei*

---

[51] Pico, *De hominis dignitate . . . e scritti varia,* ed. E. Garin (Florence, 1942),
p. 498, cited in Eugene F. Rice, *The Renaissance Idea of Wisdom* (Cambridge, Mass.,
1958), p. 67.
[52] *Summa,* I, Q. 12, a. 4. See also *The Second Anniversary,* lines 440–42 and notes.
Cf. Joannes Reuchlin, *De Arte Cabalistica* in Pietro Galatino, *De Arcanis Catholicae
Veritatis* (Basileae, 1561), p. 495: "Mens enim in homine Deus appellatur, instar
mentis summae ac primae, aut per homonymian, aut per participationem."

visae), because he saw God through a certain spiritual light infused
into the human mind from heaven, which was, as it were, an ex-
pressed likeness of increate light. . . . The second kind of sight
(*visio*) . . . is natural to angels: but it is above the nature of man.
Therefore to arrive at it man needs the light of grace.[53]

According to Donne,

we are made partakers of the divine nature . . . ; not that we are
so derived from the nature and essence of God, as that our souls
should be of his very substance . . . ; But this transmutation is a
glorious restoring of Gods image in us . . . which admits no re-
transmutation . . . ; for as a spirit cannot be divided, so they who
are thus changed into him, are so much His, so much He, that nothing can separate them from him [*Sermons*, I, 164].

The man who wrote the *Songs and Sonets* knew that "Love is
a Possessory Affection, it delivers over him that loves into the
possession of that that he loves; it is a transmutatory Affection,
it changes him that loves, into the very nature of that that he
loves, and he is nothing else" (*Sermons*, I, 184–185).

The second major strand of tradition began with the wisdom
literature of the Old Testament and the Apocrypha. In the Book
of Proverbs, wisdom is personified as a woman who was with
God from the beginning:

The Lord possessed me in the beginning of his way, before his
works of old.

I was set up from everlasting, from the beginning, or ever the
earth was.

When there were no depths, I was brought forth; when there
were no fountains abounding with water.

Before the mountains were settled, before the hills was I brought
forth: . . .

Then was I by him, as one brought up with him: and I was daily
his delight, rejoicing always before him.   [8:22–25, 30]

[53] Aquinas, *De Veritate*, Q. 18, a. 1.

The implication is that she was necessary for creation; through intercourse with her, God produced the world.

> For she is the breath of the power of God,
> And a pure emanation of his almighty glory;
> Therefore nothing defiled can enter into her.
> For she is a reflection of the everlasting light,
> And a spotless mirror of the activity of God,
> And a likeness of his goodness.
> Though she is one, she can do all things,
> And while remaining in herself, she makes everything new.
> And passing into holy souls, generation after generation,
> She makes them friends of God and prophets.
>   [The Wisdom of Solomon 7:25–27]

The personification later went two separate ways. One was its continuation in Hebrew tradition and its association with the Shekinah; the other, its transformation in Christianity.

Originated at the close of the biblical canon, the term Shekinah (*lit.*, neighborhood, abiding) was used in the Talmud to signify a nebulous being who was both Jehovah and at the same time something distinct from him representing his activity in the world and his indwelling among the children of Israel. It was an expression of the feeling common among Jews that the spirit of God, his activity in the world, is somehow different from God himself—the Ruach in Genesis and Isaiah, for example, the figure of Wisdom in Proverbs and the Apocrypha, the Logos of Philo Judaeus and Maimonides, the Memrā in the Targum, and the Metatron and the Shekinah in other rabbinical books.[54] As Edwyn Bevan has pointed out, it was an attempt to bridge the gap between the complete transcendence of God and his immanence.[55] It is impossible to pin it down any more precisely than that; it was vague even to the Jews themselves. It was not a metaphysical distinction, but a feeling: an attitude toward God that was never brought to the level of articulate realization.

[54] Edwyn Bevan, *Symbolism and Belief* (Boston, 1957), pp. 178–79.
[55] *Ibid.*, pp. 177–206.

In the cabala, however, the term was used much differently. What before was indistinct uncertainty became realized as a female element within the deity. Like the figure of Wisdom, she was God's consort, "the Daughter, Queen and Bride of light," but unlike her, she was an actual hypostasis, not a personified attribute. As the last sephirath in the cabalistic system of emanations, she is God's immanence in the world, the point where he touches matter and reveals his glory. But she is also the part of man's own soul that turns him to God:

> God in the most deeply hidden of His manifestations, which He has as it were just decided to launch upon His work of Creation, is called 'He.' God in the complete unfolding of His Being, Grace, and Love, in which He becomes capable of being perceived by the 'reason of the heart,' and therefore of being expressed, is called 'You.' But God, in His supreme manifestation, where the fullness of His Being finds its final expression in the last and all-embracing of His attributes, is called 'I.' . . . This Divine Self, this 'I,' according to the theosophical Kabbalists . . . is the Shekhinah, the presence and immanence of God in the whole Creation. It is the point where man, in attaining the deepest understanding of his own self, becomes aware of the presence of God. And only from there, standing as it were at the gate of the Divine Realm does he progress into the deeper regions of the Divine, into His 'You' and 'He' and into the depths of Nothing.[56]

Through sin man cut himself off from the Shekinah, but in so doing he also cut her off from the rest of the divine hierarchy. Abraham Halevi, for example, a disciple of the Jewish mystic David ben Luria, saw her at the Wailing Wall in Jerusalem dressed like a widow in black weeping for the lost husband of her youth.[57] The entire doctrine, known as the Exile of the Shekinah, is surrounded by doubts and hesitations. It is clear that the actual substance of God was not disturbed, but at the same

---

[56] Gershom G. Scholem, *Major Trends in Jewish Mysticism* (Jerusalem, 1941), pp. 212–13.

[57] *Ibid.*, pp. 226–27.

time it was an interruption of his inner life as well as his activity in the world. According to Joseph Gikatila:

> In the beginning of Creation, the core of the Shekinah was below, heaven and earth were one and in perfect harmony. The well springs and the channels through which everything in the higher regions flows into the lower were still active, complete and unhindered, and thus God filled everything from above to below. But when Adam came and sinned, the order of things was turned into disorder, and the heavenly channels were broken.[58]

Kingdom was separated from Foundation; man was cut off from intercourse with God.[59] But he was not left entirely alone, for the Shekinah remained with him as a part of his own nature. Man need but enter into himself in order to proceed through the Shekinah into the depths of the divine.

Among the Christian cabalists of the Renaissance, the Shekinah was variously interpreted. To some she was an archangel, the intelligence of the *primum mobile*. To others she was God himself, either the Straight Line of the cabala, the last *Midah*, which contained the influence of all the sephiroth, or the Supreme Crown, *Cheter Elion*, from which the sephiroth derived. To still others she was the mysterious Tetragrammaton whose "Ecliptic . . . is the name which presides over the first Archetypal Heaven." [60] She was the presence of the deity, the inspiration

---

[58] *Ibid.*, pp. 227–28. See also Reuchlin, *De Arte Cabalistica, op. cit.*, p. 450.

[59] Pico, *Conclusiones Cabalisticae*, 4: "Peccatum Adae fuit truncatio regni à caeteris plantis." See also Paul Ricci, cited by Joseph Blau, *The Christian Interpretation of the Cabala in the Renaissance* (New York, 1944), p. 72: "But when . . . at the stimulation of the serpent and Eve, he ate of the tree of knowledge of good and evil, . . . he separated Kingdom from Foundation; he was expelled with his offspring from the garden of pleasure, and (by dictate of the Law), he could achieve only seven sephiroth."

[60] Marin Mersenne, *L'Impiété des Déistes* (Paris, 1624), II, 410–13. In the Christian cabala the term *Shekinah* is somewhat rare. It is more generally known as *Adonai*, its masculine counterpart in the system of divine syzygies within the sephiroth. At the same time the feminine aspects were not entirely suppressed. They appear alongside the masculine and create a strange, unconscious sense of hermaphroditism. Reuchlin, for example, speaks of Adonai, the mystery of the Tetragrammaton, the ineffable Name of God:

of Moses and the prophets, and the visible form (*tanquam signo
visibili*) in which God dwelt (*habitavit*) among men.[61] But in
general she was identified in Christian terms as the Holy Ghost
or the Spirit of the Messiah: the grace of God, that was lost in
the fall and restored by the coming of Christ.[62] As such she was
identified with the World Soul, the spirit that moved over the
face of the waters at the first creation.[63] She was the immanence

the spirit, *soul*, promise (*votum*), the mystery of faith, *the mother of sons*, the
King sitting on the throne of compassion, . . . marvelous light, the last day,
the fifty gates, the day of appeasement, *the interior voice, the river flowing
from paradise*, the Second Letter of the Tetragrammaton, repentance, *the depth
of the waters, my sister, daughter of my father* (*op. cit.*, p. 523; italics mine).

In one of its aspects it is associated with the First Archetypal Heaven and the total
transcendence of the *En Soph*, "in fontani luminibus inaccessibili abysso se retrahens
& contegens" (p. 452). But at the same time it is also the last of the sephiroth, the
point of immanence, the point of entry into the divine: "Kingdom, life, . . . the
Church of Israel, the Bride in the Song of Songs, the Queen of Heaven, the Virgin
Israel, . . . the Fourth Letter of the Tetragrammaton, . . . the Temple of the
King, the door to God, . . . the Lord of the universal earth (*vniuersae terrae*)"
(p. 524). Agrippa gives virtually the same information, adding, however, a reference
to *Issim* which would seem to be particularly relevant to Elizabeth Drury:

The tenth name is *Adonai melech*, that is, lord and king: and its numeration
(*numeratio*) is *Malchuth*, which is, kingdom and empire, and signifies the
church and the temple of God and the door: and it flows through the order
(*ordinem*) *animasticum*, that is to say, the souls of the blessed, which is called
by the Jews *Issim*, that is, nobles, heroes and princes: and they are inferior to
the Hierarchies and insinuate (*influunt*) knowledge into the sons of men, and
they impart a wonderful diligence and knowledge of things and prophecy: and
the soul of the Messiah presides over them, or (as others say) the [spheral]
intelligence Metattron, which is called the first creature, or the world soul, and
the preceptor of Mosis (*Opera* [Lugduni, 1531], pp. 333–34).

Donne apparently referred to it in his sermons: "that Lord who is presented heere
not as *Jehovah* the Lord of essence and beinge, and so in his generall providence and
sustayninge of all creatures, but as *Adonai*, a Lord that is the basis and foundation
of his Church" (II, 160).

[61] Christianus Schoettgenius, *Horae Hebraicae et Talmudicae in Universum Novum
Testamentum* (Dresdae et Lipsiae, 1733), p. 1217.

[62] *Biblia latina, cum postillis Nicolai de Lyra et additionibus Pauli Burgensis*
(Nuremberg, 1497), I, fol. 26ᵛ; Reuchlin, *De Arte Cabalistica*, pp. 459–61; Galatino,
op. cit., pp. 41–43; J. H. Hottinger, ΚΤΙΣΙΣ ΕΞΑΗΜΕΡΟΣ: *Id est; Historiae
Creationis Examen* (Heidelbergae, 1659), p. 42.

[63] E.g., Mersenne, *op. cit.*, pp. 411–12; Benedictus Pererius Valentinus, *Commentariorum et Disputationum in Genesim* (Venetii, 1607), pp. 23–24; Hottinger, pp. 40–
44; *Sermons*, IX, 99–100.

of God, the "ideata Idea" of all living things, which fostered and sustained them, as well as the spirit of grace and devotion that descended on the House of David and inspired the Apostles with tongues of fire. She was the supernatural spirit of love within the human heart: "this love (*dilectionem*) or charity is the *sechina*, that is, the divinity or glory of God himself." [64] According to Guillaume Postel she was associated with the intuitive, subconscious mind of man—"the passive or material intellect," "the general basis of reason"—as opposed to the active, formal intellect, which he thought of as belonging to the father:

> And since the highest authority of the highest form, or man, corresponds to the Intellect, and the highest power of reasoning truly, the source (*fons*) of Prudence and Justice, corresponds to the lower Reason, it is necessary to think of the former as associated with the Father (*Paternitatem*), the latter with the Mother (*Maternitatem*).[65]

In more orthodox terms she was the inspiration of the Holy Ghost:

> Christ tells us things in *darknesse* [Donne wrote]; And so Christ speaks to us in our *Ear;* And these low voices, and holy whisperings, and halfe-silences, denote to us, the inspirations of his Spirit, *as his Spirit beares witnesse with our Spirit;* as the Holy Ghost insinuates himselfe into our soules, and works upon us so, by his *private motions* [*Sermons*, VII, 396].

Within orthodox Christianity the tradition of Wisdom was never very important. The woman who was with God in the beginning of his ways was usually identified allegorically as Christ, but it was obviously a thing of the mind, not the heart —an attempt to explain an otherwise obscure Jewish fable. To Christians the truth of Christianity was the truth clearly revealed, whereas the Old Testament figure of Wisdom was only a type: a mythical, poetic shadow of that truth. Whatever sur-

---

[64] Galatino, *op. cit.*, p. 42.
[65] *Apologia pro Serveto*, cited in Bouwsma, p. 145.

vived therefore in Christianity survived only in an abstract, theological form. The genuinely symbolic aspects of the image dropped out, but the image itself remained, idealized, subdivided, but nevertheless part of the theological tradition of the Church and therefore capable of being given flesh and translated back into its original symbolic form by mystics, like Jacob Boehme, or poets, like Dante and Donne.

In theology the tradition consists primarily of a distinction between the wisdom of God, perfect and utterly unknowable except insofar as it has made itself known, and the lesser wisdom of man, which is not innately his, but a supernatural gift, *de sursum descendens*. One was known technically as *sapientia increata*, the other as *sapientia creata*. As Donne explained in one of his sermons,

> The Person that professes love in this place [Proverbs 8:17] is wisdom her self, as appears at the beginning of the Chapter; so that *sapere et amare*, to be wise and to love, which perchance never met before nor since, are met in this text: but whether this wisdom, so frequently mentioned in this book of *Proverbs*, be *sapientia creata* or *increata*, whether it be the vertue wisdom, or the root of wisdom, Christ Jesus, hath been diversly debated: the occasion grew in that great Councel of *Nice*, where the Catholick Fathers understood this wisdom, to be intended of Christ himself, and then the Arrian hereticks passed some places of this book, where such things seemed to them to be spoken of wisdom, as could not be applyable to any but to a Creature; and that therefore if Christ were this wisdom, Christ must necessarily be a Creature, and not God [*Sermons*, I, 238–39].

According to Augustine, who wrote shortly after the Council of Nicaea, it was the difference between the "light that illuminates and that is illuminated." "For the intellectual nature . . . by the contemplation of light, is light" (*Confessions*, XII, 15).

Sapientia increata was traditionally associated with the metaphysical procession of the Trinity and the events of the first creation. There were two kinds: *communis*, which referred to the total Wisdom of God in all three persons, and *notabilis*, which referred specifically to the second person of the Trinity, hypostatically the Wisdom of the Father.[66] "Christ who is *Sapientia Dei*, the wisdome of God," according to Donne, "is *Verbum*, *Sermo Dei*, the word of God, he is the wisdome, and the uttering of the wisdome of God" (*Sermons*, II, 228). Like the Shekinah the increate wisdom of God was a hypostasis of God himself, but it was also in some inexplicable way a cosmic force, the creative energy of God: the point at which the Father moved out of himself into the creation. It was the first step from utter transcendence to immanence. But beyond that it was vague and ultimately mysterious as the Trinity itself. It was inherent in created things, in the order and proportion of the world. But at the same time it was ultimately incomprehensible to man. Even the imagery used to explain it was vague and confused. Christ was traditionally masculine; Wisdom was traditionally feminine; and the imagistic combination was a strange, inchoate hermaphroditism, as here; *sapientia increata* is speaking in a vision to one of its disciples:

> If þou wolt wite þe properte and resone of my name, þou schalt vnderstande þat I am clepede of hem þat livene in erþe euerlastynge wisdam, . . . ffor . . . (þe) bylouede sone of þe fadere is takene z vnderstande in þat-manere significacione of wisdam custumablye, nowe as godde z nowe as manne, nowe as he þat is spowse of his chirche z nowe as sche þat is spowse z wyfe of euerye chosene sowle.[67]

The hermaphroditism is not itself imagistic, however, but simply an indication that the two traditions never really merged except theologically. In fact, they seem to have split even further. *Sapientia increata* remained primarily Christian in imagery; as Christ, it was generally spoken of as a masculine force, whereas

[66] Cornelius à Lapide, *Commentarius in Librum Sapientiae* (Antuerpiae, 1696), p. 152, who cites Augustine, Ambrose, and Aquinas; see also his *Commentaria in Salomonis Proverbia* (Antuerpiae, 1681), p. 178.

[67] Henry Suso, *Orologium Sapientiae, or The Seven Poyntes of Trewe Wisdom*, ed. K. Horstmann, *Anglia*, X (1888), 329.

sapientia creata—"sche þat is spowse z wyfe of euerye chosene sowle"—was primarily Hebraic. It was always spoken of as a woman. *Sapientia creata* was technically defined as a participation in the uncreated Wisdom of God:

> We say that good men participate in goodness, which is God, and wise men in wisdom, which is God, because the goodness by which formally (*formaliter*) we are good is a certain participation in the divine goodness and the wisdom by which we are wise is a certain participation in the divine wisdom.[68]

It was an indwelling of the spirit of God in the mind and heart of man—a form of wisdom not acquired by the intellect, but intuitively, through grace: "The wisdom that is regarded as (*ponitur*) a gift of the Holy Ghost is different from that which is regarded as the acquired excellence (*virtus*) of the intellect. For one is acquired by human effort; the other, however, 'descends from above,' according to James 3:15" (*Summa*, II–II, Q. 45, a. 1). It was not simply the intellectual perception of God, as philosophers had said, but a direction of life, an inclination of the heart:

> Since . . . wisdom is the knowledge (*cognitio*) of divine things, it is considered differently by us and by philosophers. For our life is ordained for the ultimate enjoyment of divine things and guided by a certain participation in the divine nature, through grace. Therefore wisdom for us should be considered not only the knowledge of God, as it is among philosophers, but also as a direction of human life, which is guided not only by the impulses of the human mind (*rationes humanas*), but also by impulses of the divine, as is clear in Augustine, *De Trinitate*, XII [*Summa*, II–II, Q. 19, a. 7].

According to Donne, who, unlike Aquinas, used both terms of the ancient Stoic definition: "The Image of the second Person,

---

[68] Aquinas, *Summa*, II–II, Q. 23, a. 2; see also *Summa contra Gentiles*, IV, 9. I am considerably indebted in the discussion that follows to Charles S. Singleton's excellent *Dante Studies 2: Journey to Beatrice* (Cambridge, Mass., 1958).

whose Attribute is Wisdome, I have in this, that Wisdome being the knowledge of this world, and the next, I embrace nothing in this world, but as it leads me to the next; . . . for, here our best Wisdome is, but to goe towards our end, there it is to rest in our end; here it is to seek to bee Glorified by God, there it is, that God may be everlastingly glorified by mee" (*Sermons*, IX, 87, 89–90). It was a union of love,[69] the advent of Christ in the mind:

> The advent of Christ in the mind is through grace, producing grace (*per gratiam gratum facientem*). . . . The advent of God is not to be understood thus, that he comes where he was not already, but that he exists in a new way where he already was. For the new way by which God is in the rational creature is as the known in the knower and the loved in the lover. But, to know God and to love God as the object of beatitude is through grace, producing grace. The advent of Christ in the mind, therefore, must be understood as grace, producing grace. For that reason the wise man desired this advent when he said (*Wisdom*, IX): 'Send her forth from your holy heavens and from the throne (*sede*) of your glory, that she may be with me and labor with me.' . . . Which is as much as to say: Send Christ, the power (*virtutem*) of God and the wisdom of God, that he may be with me through the power of sanctifying grace (*gratiae gratificantis*), and that he may work with me through the love (*dilectionem*) of uplifting grace, that I may know that I am acceptable to you through the splendor of illuminating grace.[70]

Imagistically, it was the biblical figure of Wisdom, or, in Jacob Boehme's terms, the "noble Virgin Sophia," who "cometh to the Soul, and kisseth it with her sweetest *Love* in the *Essence* most inwardly, and impresseth her *Love* into its *Desire*":

> *When Christ* the *Corner-stone* stirreth Himself in the *extinquished Image* of Man, in his hearty *Conversion* and *Repentence*;

[69] Cf. *Aquinas, III Sent.*, d. XXXV, q. 2, a. 1.

[70] Aquinas, *Opusculum*, LIII, 24, cited in Singleton, p. 78. I have altered the translation slightly. See also *Summa*, II–II, Q. 23, a. 2; Bernard, *PL* 183, 43–47; Hugh of St. Victor, *PL* 175, 587; *Biblia latina, cum postillis*, II, 247ʳ; Michael Jermin, *Paraphrasticall Meditations* (London, 1638), p. 178; *Sermons*, II, 261.

the *Virgin Sophia* appeareth in the *stirring* of the *Spirit of Christ*, in the *extinguished Image*, in her *Virgin's Attire* before the Soul. At which the Soul is so amazed and astonished in its *Uncleanness*, that all its *Sins* immediately awake in it, and it trembleth before her. . . . But the *Noble Sophia* draweth near in the *Essence* of the Soul, and *kisseth* it in friendly Manner, and tinctureth its *dark Fire* with her *Rays* of *Love*, and shineth through it with her bright and powerful *Influence*. Penetrated with the strong Sense and Feeling of which, the Soul skippeth in its Body for great *Joy*, and in the Strength of this *Virgin* Love, exulteth, and praiseth the great God, for his blessed Gift of *Grace* . . . ; the Soul joineth Hands and danceth with *Sophia* or the *Divine Wisdom*.[71]

She was the Queen of Heaven, the image of God that died in Adam,[72] "the precious *Humanity of Christ*, wherein the *two Lovers*, the *Soul* and the *Humanity of Christ*, receive and embrace one another with *Joy*." [73] "For this is the *Flower* in *Sharon*, the *Rose* in the *Valley* of *Jerico*, wherewith *Solomon* delighted himself, and termed it his *dear Love*, his *chaste Virgin* which he loved; as indeed all other Saints before and after him did; whosoever obtained her, called her his *Pearl*." [74]

But the best example and perhaps the closest analogue to the *Anniversaries* is the image of Beatrice—"the now glorious lady of my mind"—as she appeared to Dante on the summit of Mount Purgatory. The story is well known. In the *Vita Nuova* Dante describes how he loved Beatrice with a surpassing love. After her death the entire world was desolate and void: "I no longer knew where I was. . . . I seemed to see the sun darken. . . ." But later she returned to him in a miraculous vision:

There appeared to me a miraculous vision in which I saw things that made me resolve to say no more about this blessed one until I should

[71] Jacob Boehme, *The Way to Christ* (Bath, 1775), pp. 36; 55–56. This was the only work of Boehme's published in his lifetime. It first appeared in 1622 and was translated into English in 1654.

[72] *Ibid.*, pp. 25–26.

[73] *Ibid.*, p. 280.

[74] *Ibid.*, p. 27.

be capable of writing about her in a more worthy fashion. And to achieve this I am striving as hard as I can, and this she truly knows. So that, if it be the wish of Him in whom all things flourish that my life continue for a few years, I hope to write of her that which has never been written of any other lady. And then may it please that One who is the Sire of Graciousness that my soul ascend to behold the glory of its lady, that is of that blessed Beatrice, who in glory gazes upon the contenance of the One *who is through all ages blessed.*[75]

It was from the perspective of that vision that he wrote the *Vita Nuova,* and it was to explain it that he began the *Divine Comedy.*

After ascending Mount Purgatory, Dante, or, in the allegory of the poem, every man who makes the interior journey of purgation, arrives at the beatitude of the summit and finds himself restored to the eternal spring of Eden. Across the stream of Lethe he perceives Matilda—in Thomistic terminology, original justice—singing and gathering flowers like Proserpine before she and the spring itself were lost. But the goal of his journey is Beatrice, the bearer of beatitude, who appears to him clothed in the infused theological virtues he has now attained. Literally she is Beatrice Portinari, the woman he once loved on earth, but within the allegory of the poem she is sanctifying grace, *sapientia creata de sursum descendens,* to the man who struggled to attain her:

> sopra candida vel cinta d'oliva
> donna m'apparve, sotto verde manto
> vestita di color di fiamma viva.
>
> [Canto xxx, 31–33]

> [a woman appeared to me in a white veil
> crowned with olive, wearing a green mantle
> and clothed in the color of living flame.]

According to the earliest commentators on the poem, she is *la celeste sapienza,* a form of wisdom unknown to the ancients:

[75] *La Vita Nuova,* trans. Mark Musa (New Brunswick, N.J., 1957), pp. 44; 85–86.

La corona d'oliva ch'è l'arbore di Minerva dea della scienze, dinotu in Beatrice la sapienza; il *bianco* del *velo*, il *verdo* del *manto*, e il *rosso* della *veste*, sono i colori attributi alle tre virtu teologali: e dei medesimi perciò ricuopre *la celeste sapienza*.[76]

She signifies the life of Christian contemplation,[77] and when she later unveils her face and reveals herself fully to Dante, she pierces his soul with a ray of the divine light. For her beauty is itself the *rerum humanarum, divinarumque scientia* that constitutes wisdom:

Beatrice has a two-fold beauty. The first has to do (*tractat*) with earthly things (*rebus humanis*), such as virtues and vices . . . : the second has to do with divine and highest things (*divinis et altissimis*), such as God and the angels; and it is that beauty that Beatrice shows him here, all at once, mingled together (*in confuso*), which shortly afterwards he perceives bit by bit, in order, as it appears constantly increasing (*crescentem*) in Paradise. . . . Therefore he says: O *splendor di viva luce eterna,* that is, O Beatrice, you are a ray of the divine light.[78]

Quae es quidam radius divinae lucis.

IV

Considered in terms of the tradition of Wisdom, certain things about the *Anniversaries* become immediately clear. I have already mentioned the fundamental structure of the poems, the alternation of contempt and glorification based on the definition

[76] Baldassarre Lombardi, cited in *La Divina Commedia,* ed. G. Biagi, G. L. Passerini, E. Rostagno (Torino, 1931), II, 643–44; see also 637, 638, 641, 642, 644 for almost identical statements by Pietro di Dante, Giovanni da Serravalle, Jacopo della Lana, Francesco da Buti, and Raffaello Andreoli. The distinction between *scienze* and *sapienza* is extremely important, as will be clear later.

[77] Cristoforo Landino, Bernardo Daniello, and Alessandro Vellutello, cited in *La Divina Commedia,* ed. Biagi *et al.,* II, 658–59.

[78] Benevenutus de Imola, *Commentum super Dantis Aldigherij Comoediam,* ed. Jacobus P. Lacaita (Florentiae, 1887), IV, 240.

of wisdom as "the right valuation of this world, and of the next."
As Donne explained in *The First Anniversary*, the purpose of
the poem was to demonstrate to the "new world"

> The dangers and diseases of the old:
> For with due temper men do then forgoe,
> Or couet things, when they their true worth know.
>
> [88–90]

The tradition also explains why the poems were written in
the form of traditional Ignatian meditations. As Louis L. Martz
has pointed out, each of the *Anniversaries* is divided into various
large structural units, or meditations, each of which in turn is
divided into three main parts. In *The First Anniversary* they are:
(1) a meditation on the decay of the world and the effects of
original sin on man and the entire frame of the universe; (2)
a eulogy of Elizabeth Drury as a lost pattern of virtue; and (3)
a refrain and moral, urging us to forget this crippled, dying
world. Martz's divisions, I think, are entirely correct, but what
he has failed to notice, though he mentions it in other parts of
his book,[79] is that these three recurrent parts of the poem correspond to the three traditional parts of the rational soul—
memory, understanding, and will. In what Martz terms the
meditations, Donne sends his mind back in time toward Eden.
Through the tradition of the decay of the world, which, as a
tradition, represents the collective memory of man, he "remem-
bers" imaginatively the perfection of the first days of the earth
and searches out the cause for the present decay. He then turns
to the intellect. In the so-called *eulogies*, he probes the significance of a young girl's recent death and discovers in it an answer
to what caused the decay. She is a way of comprehending the
lost perfection of man's soul, the grace of God in Paradise—not
logically, but emotionally, in symbolic terms. And finally, from
this combination of memory and understanding, Donne arrives
at an act of will: to forget this rotten world now that she is
dead.

[79] Martz, *op. cit.*, pp. 34–36.

The most important of these three recurrent parts of the poem is the last, the ultimate act of will; for the will, as Donne pointed out in his sermons, has a certain *Virtus transformativa:* "by it we change our selves into that we love most" (*Sermons,* IX, 373):

> *Primus actus voluntatis est Amor:* Philosophers and Divines agree in that, That the will of man cannot be idle, and the first act that the will of man produces, is Love; for till it love something, prefer and chuse something, till it would have something, it is not a Will; neither can it turn upon any object, before God. So that this first, and general, and natural love of God, is not begotten in my soul, nor produced by my soul, but created and infus'd with my soul, and as my soul; there is no soul that knows she is a soul, without such a general sense of the love of God [*Sermons,* VI, 361].

It echoes in the very first lines of the poem:

> For who is sure he hath a soule, vnlesse
> It see, and Iudge, and follow worthinesse,
> And by Deedes praise it?   [3–5]

And ultimately that is what the *Anniversaries* perform. They detach our love from this world and direct it toward the next, toward the luminous "Idea of a Woman," who represents the image of God in man.

But the will is not capable of acting alone. "All sin is from the perverseness of the will," Donne noted, but "all disorder in the will [is] from errour in the understanding" (*Sermons,* VIII, 364–365). All three faculties of the soul must flow together to form one total act of love, for all three were thought to be analogous to the Trinity, though three, yet one. In traditional Augustinian psychology the memory, understanding, and will constitute potentially the Image of God in man. When directed toward their proper goal, they enter into what they love and restore the lost likeness of the soul to God. They become in themselves Wisdom, *sapientia creata*, the image of the increate Wisdom of God:

> The Trinity in the mind itself is the Image of God, by which it re-members, understands, and loves God—which is true wisdom (*sapientia*). This Trinity of the mind therefore is the Image of God not because the mind remembers, understands, and loves itself, but because it remembers, understands, and loves the one by whom it was made. When it does that, it is wise (*sapiens*). If it does not, . . . it is stupid (*stulta*). . . . In brief, it should worship the uncreated God, who made it capable of himself (*cujus ab eo capax est facta*) and capable of being a partaker of himself (*et cujus particeps esse potest*); according to which it is written, 'Behold, the love of God (*Dei cultus*), that is wisdom' (*Job*, 28:28). And not by its own light, but by participation in the highest light will it become wise, and where eternal, there will it reign blessed.[80]

It is impossible to express in discursive language, but at this point it becomes apparent that the tripartite structure of the *Anniversaries* is identical with the central symbol that rises from it. Put into Aristotelian terms, it is the same as the relationship between efficient and final cause. The symbol is the principle because of which the poem moves toward the production of its effect. It is the form. But at the same time, seen from a slightly different perspective, the symbol is also the process itself that produces the effect. It is both the object and the wit. More concretely, if through the process of the poem—the threefold act of memory, understanding, and will—we arrive at the right valuation of this world and the next, we will have achieved within ourselves the Image of God that was lost. Our souls will have become transformed into the mysterious symbol at the center of the poem:

> Love is a Possessory Affection, it delivers over him that loves into the possession of that that he loves; it is a transmutatory Affection,

---

[80] Augustine, *De Trinitate*, PL 42, 1047. The quotation from Job (*Dei cultus*) is usually translated "fear of the Lord," but Augustine apparently did not understand it as such. Cf. PL 37, 1760: "Ecce pietas est sapientia, Θεοσεζεια dicta est in graeco; quod ut totum latine exprimatur, Dei cultus dici potest."

it changes him that loves, into the very nature of that that he loves, and he is nothing else [*Sermons*, I, 184–185].

In the second place, the tradition of Wisdom helps put into proper perspective the celebrated "new philosophy" section of *The First Anniversary*:

> And new Philosophy cals all in doubt,
> The Element of fire is quite put out;
> The Sunne is lost, and th'earth, and no mans wit
> Can well direct him, where to looke for it.
> And freely men confesse, that this world's spent,
> When in the Planets, and the Firmament
> They seeke so many new; they see that this
> Is crumbled out againe to his Atomis.
> 'Tis all in pieces, all cohaerence gone;
> All iust supply, and all Relation.   [205–214]

The passage is usually taken out of context to illustrate the impact of scientific rationalism on the Medieval world picture and the consequent unsettling of the Renaissance mind. "Donne," according to Douglas Bush, echoing Coffin, Nicolson, and others, "is wandering between two worlds, that of cosmic unity and that of meaningless disorder and decay, and he cannot resolve the conflict." [81] Such a conflict undoubtedly stands somewhere behind the *Anniversaries*—as it does behind every other poem in the Renaissance—and helps explain why they were written. But it is not the statement that the poems themselves make. The *Anniversaries* are not simply a symbolic action, an elaborate gesture of intellectual despair.

Nor, on the other hand, are they Menippian satires, as Northrop Frye recently claimed: "where the death of a girl expands into a general satire or 'anatomy'." [82] In Frye's elaborate and suggestive system of genres the anatomy, or Menippian sa-

---

[81] *English Literature in the Earlier Seventeenth Century*, 1600–1660 (Oxford, 1945), p. 132.
[82] *Anatomy of Criticism: Four Essays* (Princeton, 1957), p. 298.

tire, is directed not against people themselves, but against mental attitudes or types—"Pedants, bigots, cranks, parvenus, virtuosi, enthusiasts, rapacious and incompetent professional men of all kinds." Evil and absurdity are regarded not as moral or social phenomena, but intellectual, "a kind of maddened pedantry which the *philosophus gloriosus* at once symbolizes and defines." According to this view, Donne overwhelms "his pedantic targets with an avalanche of their own jargon." [83] He hoists them on their own petard by using the most famous discoveries of the day only to prove the decay of the world. The new medicine of Paracelsus, for example, is equated with the new disease of syphilis:

> With new diseases on our selues we warre,
> And with new phisicke, a worse Engin farre.
>
> [159–160]

And of course Frye is correct. *The First Anniversary* is shot through with satire of that sort. But again the danger is in reading the part for the whole: a complexity of tone for formal satire. The *Anniversaries* contain satire, but they are not themselves contained by it. In terms of Renaissance poetic theory they are formal *epitaphia*, one *recens*, the other, *anniversarium*, written in the mode of Ignatian meditations.

There is, however, a third alternative, which subsumes the previous two. For if the *Anniversaries* are a lament for the loss of Wisdom, *sapientia creata*, then the learning of the new philosophy as well as Donne's own hypothetical disillusion are simply forms of false wisdom that stand in contrast to it. Instead of proving the glory of man, they reveal only further the hideous deformity and decay of the world:

> Those therefore who are wise in and concerning visible things (as
> are all those outside the Faith and those who are ignorant of God
> and a future life) understand nothing and are wise in nothing, that
> is, they are neither intelligent (*intelligentes*) nor wise (*sapientes*),

[83] *Ibid.*, pp. 309; 311.

but foolish and blind. And though they may think themselves wise men, yet they have become fools. For they are wise, not in the wisdom of secret, hidden things, but of that which can be found in a human way.[84]

The distinction was traditional and ultimately goes back to Augustine:

> It is written concerning our Lord Jesus Christ that in him 'are hid all the treasures of wisdom and knowledge' (Coloss., 2:3). The eloquence of Scripture also indicates, however, that these two—that is, wisdom (sapientiam) and knowledge (scientiam)—are different from one another, and in particular the holy words of Job, where each is defined to a certain extent. For he says, 'Behold, the love of God (pietas), that is wisdom; to refrain from evil, however, is knowledge' (Job, 28:28). Not incorrectly we perceive (intelligimus) wisdom in understanding (cognitione) and in love (dilectione) of the one who always is and who remains immutable, that is God. To refrain from evil, however, which he says is knowledge, what is that but to be cautious and prudent in the midst of a crooked and perverse nation, as in the night of this century. . . .[85]

Scientia is the knowledge of this world only.[86] It is limited to what is perceived by the senses and represents the extent of man's wisdom in a state of nature.[87] Sapientia, on the other hand, is the knowledge of this world and of the next. It is a supernatural gift of God, de sursum descendens: the direct intellectual comprehension of eternal things.[88] In The Second Anniversary, for example, the satire and the agonized anatomy of the world gives way to a harmonious docta ignorantia, which forms the prelude to true wisdom:

[84] Luther, cited in Rice, The Renaissance Idea of Wisdom, p. 139; see also the entire chapter, pp. 124–48.
[85] Augustine, PL 37, 1760.
[86] PL 42, 1037.
[87] PL 40, 139.
[88] PL 42, 1012.

In this low forme, poore soule what wilt thou doe?
When wilt thou shake off this Pedantery,
Of being taught by sense, and Fantasy?
Thou look'st through spectacles; small things seeme great,
Below; But vp vnto the watch-towre get,
And see all things despoyld of fallacies:
Thou shalt not peepe through lattices of eies,
Nor heare through Laberinths of eares, nor learne
By circuit, or collections to discerne.
In Heauen thou straight know'st all, concerning it,
And what concerns it not, shall straight forget.   [290–300]

It suffuses the entire poem:

> Forget this world, and scarse thinke of it so,
> As of old cloaths, cast of a yeare agoe.
> To be thus stupid is Alacrity;
> Men thus lethargique haue best Memory.
> Looke vpward; that's towards her, whose happy state
> We now lament not, but congratulate.   [61–66]

Finally, the tradition of Wisdom helps explain the fundamental difference between the two poems: they stand in the same relation to one another as *scientia* to *sapientia*. As Donne explained in one of his sermons,

> a regenerate Christian, being now a *new Creature,* hath also *a new facultie of Reason.* . . . Divers men may walke by the Sea side, and the same beames of the Sunne giving light to them all, one gathereth by the benefit of that light pebels, or speckled shells, for curious vanitie, and another gathers precious Pearle, or medicinall Ambar, by the same light. So the common light of reason illuminates us all; but one imployes this light upon the searching of impertinent vanities, another by a better use of the same light, finds out the Mysteries of Religion; and when he hath found them, loves them. . . . Some men by the benefit of this light of Reason, have found

out things profitable and usefull to the whole world; As in particular, *Printing* . . . [and] *Artillery*, by which warres come to quicker ends then heretofore, and the great expence of bloud is avoyded. . . . But . . . their light seems to be great out of the same reason, that a Torch in a misty night, seemeth greater then in a clear, because it hath kindled and inflamed much thicke and grosse Ayre round about it. . . .

But, if thou canst take this light of reason that is in thee, this poore snuffe, that is almost out in thee, thy faint and dimme knowledge of God, that riseth out of this light of nature, if thou canst in those embers, those cold ashes, finde out one small coale, and wilt take the paines to kneell downe, and blow that coale with thy devout *Prayers*, . . . if . . . thou canst turne this little light inward, and canst thereby discerne where thy diseases, and thy wounds, and thy corruptions are, and canst apply those teares, and blood and balme to them, . . . thou shalt never envy the lustre and glory of the great lights of worldly men. . . . Their light shall set at noone; even in their heighth, . . . and thy light shall grow up, from a *faire hope*, to a modest assurance and *infallibility*, that that light shall never go out . . . ; as thy light of *reason* is exalted by *faith* here, so thy light of *faith* shall be exalted into the light of *glory*, and fruition in the Kingdome of heaven . . . ; in a man regenerate by faith, that light does all that reason did, *and more* [*Sermons*, III, 359–362].

The First Anniversary is concerned only with the light of reason, unaided by faith. Its tone, therefore, is analytic and satirical; through the use of reason it explores the limits of reason. It proceeds "punctually" from part to part in rigid logical sequence, but its overall movement is downward to decay. Its ultimate discovery is a universe of death. At the same time, however, proceeding from the operation of reason in the poem is the silent process of transformation by which the soul is changed into the very nature of that which it loves. As Donne explains toward the end of the poem, he has rewritten the Song of Moses for his own times, traditionally regarded as the complete summary of the Law, teaching the fear of the Lord and the severity of judgment.[89] It marked the furthest extent to which man could proceed by human reason alone; beyond lay the dispensation of Grace. Therefore, after delivering the Song to his people, Moses ascended Mount Nebo with the Lord and from the top of Pisgah looked over into the Promised Land. But he was not able to enter.

In *The Second Anniversary*, however, Donne crossed over, and the entire poem surges upward toward eternal life:

> Looke vpward; that's towards her, whose happy state
> We now lament not, but congratulate.   [65–66]

The meditations begin with death ("Thinke then, My soule, that death is but a Groome"), the point at which *The First Anniversary* and natural man end, and proceed beyond:

> But thinke that Death hath now enfranchis'd thee,
> Thou hast thy'expansion now and libertee;
> Thinke that a rusty Peece, discharg'd, is flowen
> In peeces, and the bullet is his owne,
> And freely flies: This to thy soule allow,
> Thinke thy sheell broke, thinke thy Soule hatch'd but now.
> [179–184]

The symbolism diminishes. Elizabeth Drury becomes more and more recognizable as an idealized pattern of virtue. For the soul itself has now attained the Wisdom that was lost. It has become internalized, and the emotions that were once concentrated within the symbol have now become diffused throughout the entire poem. The total movement of *The Second Anniversary* is harmonious and organic not, as is usually believed, because it is a success and *The First Anniversary* a failure, but because through the purgative process of *The First Anniversary* the soul has at last arrived at a right valuation of this world, and of the next, and rests secure in the love of God. As Dante

[89] Lines 461–68 and notes.

remarked, commenting on the phrase, "When Israel went out of Egypt":

> If we regard the *literal* sense alone it signifies the departure of the sons of Israel from Egypt in the time of Moses; *allegorically,* it signifies our redemption through Christ; *morally,* it signifies the conversion of the soul from the grief and misery of sin to the state of grace; *anagogically,* it signifies the departure of the blessed soul from the slavery of this corruption to the freedom of everlasting glory.[90]

V

The text is based upon the first edition of each poem, the 1611 edition of the *Anatomy of the World* and the *Funerall Elegie* and the 1612 edition of the *Progres of the Soule*. These are the only substantive texts; all other editions are derived texts only, with no independent authority. The original manuscripts are now lost, and the *Anniversaries* appear in none of the surviving manuscript collections of Donne's poetry. The only manuscript of any portion of the *Anniversaries* is a copy of the *Funerall Elegie* in the Bodleian MS. ENG. POET. e 37, which was taken directly from the 1621 edition. Presumably since the poems were in print almost immediately after they were written, there was no need for extensive manuscript circulation.

The exact date of the 1611 edition is not known; the volume was never entered on the Stationers' Register.[91] But it must have been written early in the year. Elizabeth Drury died in December, 1610, and since it was an elegy, the poem was probably written shortly afterward. It was almost certainly completed by mid-November, 1611, when Donne left England for a tour of the Continent with the Drurys, since it was presumably on the strength of the work that he was asked to accompany them. It was printed for Samuel Macham at the sign of the Bullhead

---

[90] *Opere,* ed. Moore, p. 415.

[91] Bibliographical descriptions are available in Geoffrey Keynes, *Bibliography of Dr John Donne* (Cambridge, 1958).

in Paul's Churchyard, probably by Humfrey Lownes, Senior. His name does not appear on the title page, but as Geoffrey Keynes has pointed out, an identical woodcut border printed from the same block appears on the title pages of Joseph Hall's *Passion Sermon* (1609) and *Pharisaisme and Christianitie* (1609), both of which were printed by him (*Bibliography,* p. 135). The volume is remarkably well printed, the body of the text in clear, sharp italics with the surrounding material, the *Praise of the Dead* and the *Funerall Elegie,* in ordinary roman type. Punctuation is intelligent and exact, capitalization consistent and consistently meaningful. Care is taken to see that half rimes are completed by spelling (*vpone: one*) and that full rimes similarly are spelled alike (*part: hart; much: tuch*). There are very few typographical errors, but since only two copies of the 1611 edition survive, it is impossible to say precisely how many stages the text went through in arriving at its present condition: whether its excellence is due to careful proofing or careful presswork or, as is most likely, a combination of both. All that can be said for certain is that four type chases were unlocked in press and changes made on the inner and outer forms of sheets A and B, the two gatherings composing the volume.[92] Nevertheless, taking into account its general excellence, it is tempting to believe that Donne saw it through the press himself. We know that he was extremely fastidious about such matters later in his life,[93] and since this was his first published poem, one of the few ever printed in his lifetime,[94] it seems reasonable to suppose that he would have taken some care with it. But even if Donne did not see it through the press himself, the text is still remarkably good. It is undoubtedly an accurate reproduction of the original manuscript and furnishes the only authoritative text of *The First Anniversary.*

[92] In the table of press variants at the end of the text, I have labeled some of these differences corrected, others uncorrected, but without more copies to collate it is impossible to tell. In most cases the term corrected should be taken to mean only that that is the reading adopted in the present text.

[93] E. M. Simpson, "A Note on Donne's Punctuation," *RES,* IV (1928).

[94] Besides the *Anniversaries* the only others were the commendatory verses for *Coryats Crudities* (1611) and the *Elegie* on the death of Prince Henry in Sylvester's *Lachrymae Lachrymarum* (1613).

The 1612 edition consists of a reprint of the 1611 edition along with the first printing of the *Harbinger to the Progres* and the *Progres of the Soule*. It is thus the second edition of one poem and the first edition of the other. Each part was given a separate title page, but the 1611 portion of the text was completely reset and made to conform to a new format. The type face was reversed: the body of the text was printed in roman, with the subsidiary material in italics. The text itself was placed within marginal rules, which considerably shortened the page and caused each line of verse to be printed in two half lines, thus:

> Loth to goe vp the hill, or la-
>   bor thus
> To goe to heauen, we make
>   heauen come to vs.

Marginal glosses were added to both poems, whether by Donne or by the printer is not known, and both poems were incorporated for the first time under the general heading of *Anniversaries*. As in 1611 the volume was never entered on the Stationers' Register, and the precise date is unknown. But the second part of the poem was probably begun at Amiens in December, 1611, on the first anniversary of Elizabeth Drury's death, and it was completed in France as the allusion to the "french conuertite" in lines 511–518 makes clear. The Drury party remained at Amiens from late November, 1611, to mid-March, 1612. It removed to Paris for a month and left for Frankfort in late April, 1612.[95] The poem had been sent to England and published sometime before the party left France, since Donne answered criticism of his *Anniversaries* in letters from Paris dated 12 or 14 April, 1612. The volume was again printed for Samuel Macham, not by Humfrey Lownes, but by Melchisadec Bradwood, who did a relatively inferior job. There was some attempt at press correction earlier in the volume, in the text of *The*

---

[95] R. E. Bennett, "Donne's Letters from the Continent in 1611–12," *PQ*, XIX (1940), and R. C. Bald, *Donne and the Drurys*, pp. 85–103.

First Anniversary, but there is no indication that the type chases were ever unlocked during the printing of *The Second Anniversary*. It would seem that it was simply set up and run off. And the general condition of the text would seem to support that conclusion. It is shot through with a great number of obvious typographical errors that would have been corrected by any conscientious printer. Since Donne was in France at the time of printing, he obviously could not have seen the volume through the press himself, and it is pleasant to believe that the inferior state of the text is due at least as much to the lack of authorial supervision as to the change in printer. But without further evidence nothing can be definitely proved.

A new fact, however, was recently discovered. On May 13, 1946, at Sotheby's, a copy of the 1612 edition formerly bound in with a copy of John Hall's *Poems* (1646) was purchased by Geoffrey Keynes. Pasted on the verso of H5 was an errata slip correcting twenty-eight errors in the 1612 edition: seven in *The First Anniversary*, one in the *Harbinger to the Progres*, and twenty in *The Second Anniversary*.[96] Whether Donne was personally responsible for the errata slip or whether it was drawn up by the printer as a belated gesture toward correctness is not known for certain, but it seems probable that when Donne returned from the Continent and discovered the state of the text he drew up a list of errata and demanded that Bradwood print it. That would perhaps explain the extreme rarity of the errata slip. Only one copy has survived, and even in the seventeenth century it seems to have been almost as rare, since not one later edition of the *Anniversaries* made use of it. Presumably by the time Donne returned to London in early September, 1612, most of the volumes in stock had already been sold. That would also explain some of the corrections made by the errata slip in the text of *The First Anniversary*. It is clear that Brad-

[96] The errata were printed by John Sparrow in *TLS*, 29 June, 1946. Sparrow overlooked one of the corrections, however. He failed to print the second change from *then* to *there*, in line 259 of *The First Anniversary*. And he underrated the significance of the others, believing, after Grierson, that the 1633 edition "provides the most satisfactory basis for a received text."

wood set his text directly from a copy of the 1611 edition since he reproduces scrupulously all its peculiarities and all its errors. It was, of course, standard practice for a printer to set from typescript whenever possible in order to relieve himself of the difficulties involved in composing from manuscript. Moreover, it is unlikely that Bradwood was sent a manuscript of *The First Anniversary* along with that of the *Second* or that he had one available to him through Macham. Yet the errata slip corrects four errors in the 1611 edition, which is impossible if Bradwood were proofreading against his original, and even granted that one of the corrections, the confusion of the long *s* and *f* in line 474, could have been derived from context, as it was in the 1633 edition, the other three could not. In two instances the same correction occurs: *there* is substituted for *then* in lines 217 and 259.[97] The two words would have resembled one another somewhat in seventeenth-century Secretary hand, and it is easy to see how the mistake was made. Yet if they looked enough alike to have caused confusion in the first place, it is difficult to see how anyone except the person who had written them would have been able to tell them apart with enough assurance to make a point about correcting them, especially since the substitution does not change the meaning of the line. It simply removes the slight idea of sequence that *then* creates. The correction in line 262 seems to have come about in the same way. *Towres* is changed to *Townes; r* and *n* were often confused in seventeenth-century Secretary script; but only the author would have been likely to make the correction. In context either word would have been possible, though *Townes* completes the submerged metaphor in the lines and is far the better reading. Thus, unless the printer read proof against the original manuscript of *The First Anniversary*, which is highly improbable, it seems reasonable to assume that Donne drew up the errata slip himself.

The errata slip considerably improves the text of *The Second Anniversary*, but it does not perfect it. It fails to correct a few

[97] The same correction occurs again in the errata in line 232 of *The Second Anniversary*.

obvious mistakes, such as *safe-fealing* in line 46, *worlds* in line
423, and *Thinks* in line 416. And it corrects a few others that
are of doubtful significance, such as the change from *Hydroptique* to *Hydropique* in line 48 and *to'rect* to *t'erect* in line 417.
There are a number of other substantive and semi-substantive
changes throughout the text that remain unchanged. Even so,
the errata slip stands as an important source of authority, though
it is difficult to say precisely what it represents. It is obviously
not a new, independent revision of the text; it is parasitic to
the 1612 edition; and yet it goes beyond the usual limits of an
errata slip. It corrects errors not only in the text it is immediately
attached to, but also in the text of the volume that immediately
preceded it, and there is even some reason to believe that Donne
used it to make actual revisions in the text, as is pointed out in
the note to line 338. Moreover, unlike most errata slips it stands
outside the main line of textual descent and furnishes an ironic
perspective from which to view the attempts at emendation in
later editions. In the 1612 text, for example, lines 47 and 48 of
The Second Anniversary read:

> Bee thirsty still, and drinke still till, thou goe;
> T'o th'onely Health, to be Hydroptique so.

In 1621 *T'o* was changed to *To,* and the comma was removed
after *till.* But that still left the awkward semicolon after *goe,*
until in 1633 the lines were smoothed out to:

> Bee thirsty still, and drinke still till thou goe
> To th'onely Health, to be Hydroptique so.

The errata slip, however, reads:

> Bee thirsty still, and drinke still till thou goe;
> 'Tis th'onely Health, to be Hydropique so.

In 1621 and 1625 the *Anniversaries* were reprinted for
Thomas Dewe by Augustine Matthews of Cow Lane and William

Stansby of St. Paul's Wharf. Neither of these editions has any authority. The first was printed directly from the 1612 edition and the second directly from the 1621.

In 1633, two years after Donne's death, John Mariot published the first edition of the collected poems. This is one of the most important volumes in the seventeenth century. It is the first edition of almost all of Donne's poems except the *Anniversaries,* and for most of them furnishes the best text. As both Grierson and Miss Gardner have pointed out, the editor had the assistance of a number of excellent manuscript collections, which he used with considerable care and intelligence. For the *Anniversaries,* however, he based his text directly on the 1625 reprint. Despite Grierson's assertion that the editor "compared this [the 1625 text] with earlier editions, probably those of 1611–1612," there is no evidence whatsoever that he saw any edition other than his copy-text. All of the marginal notes omitted in 1625 are also omitted in 1633. In the 1612 and 1621 texts, *The Second Anniversary,* line 96, asks the soul to consider itself "parch'd with feuers violence." In the 1625 edition *parch'd* became *pach'd.* In 1633 the editor, probably thinking of the splotches produced by fever, accepted the reading and normalized the spelling to *patch'd.* Similarly, the *Funerall Elegie,* line 33, reads, "so great as shee." Since the 1625 text lost the comparative, making it "so great shee," the editor of 1633 had no way of knowing what was wrong with the line, so he made it into a statement, "so great was shee." The 1633 is not an exact reprint of the 1625, however. The editor intended to make as good a text as possible. Consequently he corrected mistakes when he saw them, removed obsolete words, modernized old-fashioned spellings, altered capitalization, and entirely repunctuated both poems. The result was the equivalent of a modernized text with no authority whatsoever. Compared with earlier editions, it marks the greatest divergence from Donne's probable intentions.

The *Anniversaries* were reprinted in the editions of Donne's poems published in 1635, 1639, 1649, 1650 (printed from the standing type of 1649), 1654 (a reissue of the 1650 with cancel title page), and 1669. Each of these seems to have been printed

from the one immediately preceding it. At times obvious mistakes in earlier editions are corrected by context, but in general
these later editions reveal only the progressive degeneration of
the 1633 text, the ultimate basis for them all.

The *Anniversaries* were reprinted in the eighteenth century in
the edition of Donne's collected poems published by Jacob Ton-
son in 1719. The text was based directly on the 1669 version.
They were later reprinted in volume twenty-five of Bell's *Poets
of Great Britain* (1779), volume four of Anderson's *Works of
the British Poets* (1795), and volume five of Chalmers' *Works
of the English Poets* (1810). The copy-text for all these was the
1719 edition. In 1839 they were edited by Henry Alford in volume six of his edition of Donne's works. This was the first attempt to establish an accurate text. It is difficult to determine
what edition Alford used as his basic text since there is a considerable mixture of readings, but he apparently adopted either
the 1635 or 1639 with liberal variants from the 1633. James
Russell Lowell edited the *Anniversaries* in 1855 in an edition of
Donne's poems which appeared as volume thirty-nine of *The
Complete Collection of the British Poets*, edited by F. J. Child.
This also is a difficult text, but it seems to have been based on
the 1719 with collations from earlier editions, definitely the
1669 and perhaps the 1633. The first attempt at an old spelling
text was made by Alexander Grosart in his *Complete Poems of
John Donne* edited for *The Fuller Worthies' Library* in 1872.
Grosart chose the 1625 edition as his basic text, "being the last
issued during the author's lifetime." He claimed to have collated
all the printed editions "and mss.," but there is no evidence
in the sparse record of variants that he saw any other edition
except the 1669. James Russell Lowell edited the *Anniversaries*
for a second time in the edition of Donne's poems printed for
the Grolier Club in 1895.[98] The basic text was a modernized version of the 1633. Nothing earlier was regarded, even for collation, but all later editions seem to have been inspected. Only
about half of the variants are recorded, however. The last nine-

---

[98] The volume was edited by Lowell, revised by Charles Eliot Norton, with collations by Norton and Lowell's daughter.

teenth-century text of the *Anniversaries* was edited by E. K. Chambers for his *Muses' Library* edition of Donne in 1896. As Chambers explained in the notes, he was able to inspect only the 1621 and 1625 editions. He apparently modernized the 1621 as his basic text.

Sir Herbert J. C. Grierson's monumental edition of Donne appeared in 1912. Though dated and becoming increasingly obsolete, this is still the standard edition, and for its time it was a remarkable work. The text of the *Anniversaries*, however, is not based on sound principles. It was an anomaly for Grierson. For most of the poems he could rely on the first edition, the 1633, as his copy-text, corrected by the various manuscript collections. The same, of course, was not true with the *Anniversaries*, but Grierson acted as though it were. He failed to see the difference between a substantive and derived text and somehow convinced himself that although the editor of 1633 had set up from a copy of the 1625 edition, he had also examined all earlier texts and corrected and generally improved them. Grierson, therefore, based his own text on the 1633 and furthered the work of the supposed editor by freely adopting from earlier editions whatever struck his fancy. His textual apparatus, for example, gives the impression of being a complete historical collation, but is in fact only a record of the numerous changes made in the basic text. Moreover, Grierson failed to examine the first editions carefully. He admitted to Geoffrey Keynes that he had inspected the 1611 edition rather carelessly: "[Grierson] had, as he has told me, only a brief view of the book at Bridgewater House, being distracted at the time of his visit by the interesting discovery of the Bridgewater MS. of the poems. The text of the *Anatomy* was in consequence somewhat cursorily examined." [99] And he never saw a copy of the 1612 edition. As he explained in the Preface to the edition, "Almost at the eleventh hour, Mr. Geoffrey Keynes, of St. Bartholomew's Hospital, discovered for me a copy of the 1612 edition of the *Anniversaries*, for which I had asked in vain in *Notes and Queries*. I owe to him . . . a

[99] *An Anatomy of the World: A Facsimile of the First Edition, 1611* (Cambridge, 1951), p. 7.

careful collation and a photograph of the title page" (I, xiii).
The collation referred to was textual, not bibliographical.

Since Grierson, the *Anniversaries* have been edited by John
Heywood in 1929 and by Roger Bennett in 1942. Heywood
collated only the 1621 and 1625 editions; for the rest he relied
on Grierson's incomplete apparatus. Like Grierson he based his
text on the 1633 and corrected it from earlier editions according
to his own taste. Bennett, on the other hand, produced an independent text. He collated the 1611 and 1612 editions and
used them as his copy-texts, but since he intended the work for
the general public, he did not give a complete apparatus. Moreover, he negated the value of his primary texts by modernizing
spelling and punctuation throughout. In the last modern edition
to include any part of the *Anniversaries,* A. Davenport edited
the two commendatory verses, *To the Praise of the Dead* and
The Harbinger to the Progres for his *Collected Poems of Joseph
Hall* (1949). The text is excellent, but it is Hall, not Donne.

Besides editions, there have been three facsimile reproductions
of the *Anniversaries.* The first, a process-facsimile published by
Noel Douglas in 1926, reproduced the 1621 text from a copy
in the British Museum. The second was a reproduction of the
1621 text of *The First Anniversary,* published by The High
House Press in 1929, and the third, printed for the Roxburghe
Club by Geoffrey Keynes in 1951, reproduced the 1611 edition.
This last is a composite volume made up of photographs of the
best pages of the two surviving copies of the text.

The present edition is based on a collation of the following
twenty-four texts:

1611: The Henry E. Huntington Library; G. L. Keynes

1612: The Folger Shakespeare Library; Harvard University; The
Henry E. Huntington Library; G. L. Keynes; Yale University
copy 1 (wanting C1, C8, D1, D8, G3 and H3) and copy 2
(wanting D2–7)

1621: The British Museum; Harvard University

1625: Harvard University; Yale University

1633: The Folger Shakespeare Library copy 1 (7045) and copy 2 (7045a)

1635: The Folger Shakespeare Library; Harvard University

1639: The Folger Shakespeare Library; Harvard University

1649: Harvard University; The Henry E. Huntington Library

1650: The Folger Shakespeare Library

1654: The Folger Shakespeare Library

1669: The Folger Shakespeare Library; The Tudor-Stuart Club of The Johns Hopkins University [100]

The eight copies of the basic texts are the only ones known to survive and include one previously unknown, the second Yale copy of the 1612 edition, given to the University by Arthur M. Rosenbloom in 1957. In general I have followed the editorial principles established by Ronald B. McKerrow in his *Prolegomena to the Oxford Shakespeare* and Fredson T. Bowers in his edition of Dekker. The copy-texts are reproduced as exactly as possible in their original spelling and punctuation. Since *The First Anniversary* is the only poem we have any reason to believe Donne saw through the press himself, I have edited it extremely conservatively, altering it only where corrected by the errata slip or where obviously wrong. Fortunately it was an excellent text to begin with and little editorial work was necessary. The text of *The Second Anniversary* was edited a little more heavily. As I have indicated earlier, it is not particularly trustworthy, even with the errata slip, and I have not hesitated to correct it. At the same time, however, I have respected its authority and have not emended it except where a reading was obviously impossible, syntactically or otherwise. All emendations are listed in the footnotes to the text. Except for the errata slip, they are

---

[100] The dates of the editions are used as the sigla, except for the manuscript of the *Funerall Elegie* in the Bodleian Library (MS ENG. POET. e 37), for which the siglum *B* is used.

made on my own authority, but in almost all cases I have adopted the reading of the first seventeenth-century edition to correct the error. Although this is an old spelling text, I have not attempted to reproduce insignificant typographical details, such as the long *s,* the typography of the titles, various ligatures, swash forms, digraphs, and the use of *vv* for *w.* I have silently corrected broken and turned letters and run-on words, except where the error accidentally caused a substantive variant, such as *rebellions pride* for *rebellious pride.* I have also silently expanded printers' contractions, such as *w^{ch}* for *which, &* for *and, whē* for *when.* I have, on the other hand, retained the normal seventeenth-century distinction between *i* and *j* and *u* and *v.* They are easy enough to reproduce and offer no serious difficulty to the modern reader.

Variants are listed in three places. In the footnotes to the text I have indicated all emendations made in the copy-texts and identified their sources. Other than the exceptions noted above, all changes are recorded, both substantive and accidental. Second, in an appendix labeled "Historical Collation" I have listed all substantive and, in a few border line cases, semi-substantive variants found in the texts of the *Anniversaries* in the course of the seventeenth century. Such a listing seemed particularly important in this case since these are the only poems of Donne's published in his lifetime and therefore the only ones to reflect the usage of his own time and not that of twenty-five or thirty years later. It is important, I think, to be reminded of that as well as to see what sort of changes were likely to have been made in 1633. A final appendix records in tabular form all press variants found in the copy-texts.

THE FIRST ANNIUERSARIE.

AN
ANATOMY
OF THE WORLD.
WHEREIN,
BY OCCASION OF
THE VNTIMELY DEATH OF MISTRIS
ELIZABETH DRVRY
THE FRAILTY AND THE DECAY
OF THIS WHOLE WORLD
IS REPRESENTED.

To The Praise
of the Dead, and the
Anatomy.

Wel dy'de the world, that we might liue to see
This world of wit, in his Anatomee:
No euill wants his good: so wilder heyres
Bedew their fathers Toombs with forced teares,
Whose state requites their los: whils thus we gain   5
Well may we walk in blacks, but not complaine.
Yet, how can I consent the world is dead
While this Muse liues? which in his spirits stead
Seemes to informe a world: and bids it bee,
In spight of losse, or fraile mortalitee?   10
And thou the subiect of this wel-borne thought,
Thrise noble maid, couldst not haue found nor sought
A fitter time to yeeld to thy sad Fate,
Then whiles this spirit liues; that can relate
Thy worth so well to our last nephews eyne,   15
That they shall wonder both at his, and thine:
Admired match! where striues in mutuall grace
The cunning Pencill, and the comely face:

Title   The First Anniuersarie.] *1612; om. 1611*
12   maid,] *1633;* ~ ; *1611–25*

A taske, which thy faire goodnes made too much
For the bold pride of vulgar pens to tuch;   20
Enough is vs to praise them that praise thee,
And say that but enough those praises bee,
Which had'st thou liu'd, had hid their fearefull head
From th'angry checkings of thy modest red:
Death bars reward and shame: when enuy's gone,   25
And gaine; 'tis safe to giue the dead their owne.
As then the wise Egyptians wont to lay
More on their Tombs, then houses: these of clay,
But those of brasse, or marble were; so wee
Giue more vnto thy Ghost, then vnto thee.   30
Yet what we giue to thee, thou gau'st to vs,
And maist but thanke thy selfe, for being thus:
Yet what thou gau'st, and wert, O happy maid,
Thy grace profest all due, where 'tis repayd.
So these high songs that to thee suited bine,   35
Serue but to sound thy makers praise, in thine,
Which thy deare soule as sweetly sings to him
Amid the Quire of Saints and Seraphim,
As any Angels tongue can sing of thee;
The subiects differ, tho the skill agree: 40
For as by infant-yeares men iudge of age,
Thy early loue, thy vertues, did presage
What an hie part thou bear'st in those best songs
Whereto no burden, nor no end belongs.
Sing on, thou Virgin soule, whose lossefull gaine   45
Thy loue-sicke Parents haue bewayl'd in vaine;
Neuer may thy name be in our songs forgot
Till we shall sing thy ditty, and thy note.

The First Anniuersary.

An
Anatomy of
The World.

When that rich soule which to her Heauen is gone, *The entrie into the worke.*
Whom all they celebrate, who know they haue one,
(For who is sure he hath a soule, vnlesse
It see, and Iudge, and follow worthinesse,
And by Deedes praise it? He who doth not this,   5
May lodge an In-mate soule, but tis not his.)
When that Queene ended here her progresse time,
And, as t'her standing house, to heauen did clymbe,
Where, loth to make the Saints attend her long,
Shee's now a part Loth of the Quire, and Song,   10
This world, in that great earth-quake languished;
For in a common Bath of teares it bled,
Which drew the strongest vitall spirits out:
But succour'd then with a perplexed doubt,
Whether the world did loose or gaine in this,   15
(Because since now no other way there is

Title The First Anniuersary.] 1612; *om.* 1611
1 *Marginal note The entrie into the worke.*] 1612; *om.* 1611. 1611 *prints no marginal notes*

67

But goodnes, to see her, whom all would see,
All must endeuour to be good as shee,)
This great consumption to a feuer turn'd,
And so the world had fits; it ioy'd, it mournd.   20
And, as men thinke, that Agues physicke are,
And th'Ague being spent, giue ouer care,
So thou, sicke world, mistak'st thy selfe to bee
Well, when alas, thou'rt in a Letargee.
Her death did wound, and tame thee than, and than   25
Thou mightst haue better spar'd the Sunne, or Man;
That wound was deepe, but 'tis more misery,
That thou hast lost thy sense and memory.
T'was heauy then to heare thy voyce of mone,
But this is worse, that thou art speechlesse growne.   30
Thou hast forgot thy name, thou hadst; thou wast
Nothing but she, and her thou hast o'repast.
For as a child kept from the Font, vntill
A Prince, expected long, come to fulfill
The Ceremonies, thou vnnam'd hadst laid,   35
Had not her comming, thee her Palace made:
Her name defin'd thee, gaue thee forme and frame,
And thou forgetst to celebrate thy name.
Some moneths she hath beene dead (but being dead,
Measures of times are all determined)   40
But long shee'ath beene away, long, long, yet none
Offers to tell vs who it is that's gone.
But as in states doubtfull of future heyres,
When sickenes without remedy, empayres
The present Prince, they're loth it should be said,   45
The Prince doth languish, or the Prince is dead:
So mankind feeling now a generall thaw,
A strong example gone equall to law,
The Cyment which did faithfully compact
And glue all vertues, now resolu'd, and slack'd,   50

Thought it some blasphemy to say sh'was dead;
Or that our weakenes was discouered
In that confession; therefore spoke no more
Then tongues, the soule being gone, the losse deplore.
But though it be too late to succour thee,   55
Sicke world, yea dead, yea putrified, since shee
Thy'ntrinsique Balme, and thy preseruatiue,
Can neuer be renew'd, thou neuer liue,
I (since no man can make thee liue) will trie,
What we may gaine by thy Anatomy.   60
Her death hath taught vs dearely, that thou art
Corrupt and mortall in thy purest part.
Let no man say, the world it selfe being dead,
'Tis labour lost to haue discouered
The worlds infirmities, since there is none   65
Aliue to study this dissectione;
For there's a kind of world remaining still,   *What life*
Though shee which did inanimate and fill   *the world*
The world, be gone, yet in this last long night, *hath still*
Her Ghost doth walke; that is, a glimmering light,   70
A faint weake loue of vertue and of good
Reflects from her, on them which vnderstood
Her worth; And though she haue shut in all day,
The twi-light of her memory doth stay;
Which, from the carcasse of the old world, free,   75
Creates a new world; and new creatures be
Produc'd: The matter and the stuffe of this,
Her vertue, and the forme our practise is.
And though to be thus Elemented, arme
These Creatures, from hom-borne intrinsique harme,   80
(For all assum'd vnto this Dignitee,
So many weedlesse Paradises bee,
Which of themselues produce no venemous sinne,
Except some forraine Serpent bring it in)

Yet, because outward stormes the strongest breake,   85
And strength it selfe by confidence growes weake,
This new world may be safer, being told
The dangers and diseases of the old: *The sicknesses*
For with due temper men do then forgoe,   *of the world.*
Or couet things, when they their true worth know.   90
There is no health; Physitians say that we   *Impossibility*
At best, enioy, but a neutralitee.   *of health.*
And can there be worse sickenesse, then to know
That we are neuer well, nor can be so?
We are borne ruinous: poore mothers crie,   95
That children come not right, nor orderly,
Except they headlong come, and fall vpon
An ominous precipitation.
How witty's ruine? how importunate
Vpon mankinde? It labour'd to frustrate   100
Euen Gods purpose; and made woman, sent
For mans reliefe, cause of his languishment.
They were to good ends, and they are so still,
But accessory, and principall in ill.
For that first mariage was our funerall: 105
One woman at one blow, then kill'd vs all,
And singly, one by one, they kill vs now.
We doe delightfully our selues allow
To that consumption; and profusely blinde,
We kill our selues, to propagate our kinde.   110
And yet we doe not that; we are not men:
There is not now that mankinde, which was then
When as the Sunne, and man, did seeme to striue,
(Ioynt tenants of the world) who should suruiue.   *Shortnesse*
When Stag, and Rauen, and the long-liu'd tree,   *of life.* 115
Compar'd with man, dy'de in minoritee.
When, if a slow-pac'd starre had stolne away
From the obseruers marking, he might stay

Two or three hundred yeares to see't againe,
And then make vp his obseruation plaine;   120
When, as the age was long, the sise was great:
Mans grouth confess'd, and recompenc'd the meat:
So spacious and large, that euery soule
Did a faire Kingdome, and large Realme controule:
And when the very stature thus erect,   125
Did that soule a good way towards Heauen direct.
Where is this mankind now? who liues to age,
Fit to be made *Methusalem* his page?
Alas, we scarse liue long enough to trie
Whether a new made clocke runne right, or lie.   130
Old Grandsires talke of yesterday with sorrow,
And for our children we reserue to morrow.
So short is life, that euery peasant striues,
In a torne house, or field, to haue three liues.
And as in lasting, so in length is man   135
Contracted to an inch, who was a span.   *Smalenesse*
For had a man at first, in Forrests stray'd,   *of stature.*
Or shipwrack'd in the Sea, one would haue laid
A wager that an Elephant, or Whale
That met him, would not hastily assaile   140
A thing so equall to him: now alas,
The Fayries, and the Pigmies well may passe
As credible; mankind decayes so soone,
We're scarse our Fathers shadowes cast at noone.
Onely death addes t'our length: nor are we growne   145
In stature to be men, till we are none.
But this were light, did our lesse volume hold
All the old Text; or had we chang'd to gold
Their siluer; or dispos'd into lesse glas,
Spirits of vertue, which then scattred was.   150

---

129 trie∧] *1633;* ~ *;1611–25*
144 scarse] *1612 errata, 1625;* scarsc *1611*

But 'tis not so: w'are not retir'd, but dampt;
And as our bodies, so our mindes are cramp't:
'Tis shrinking, not close-weauing, that hath thus,
In minde and body both bedwarfed vs.
We seeme ambitious, Gods whole worke t'vndoe;   155
Of nothing he made vs, and we striue too,
To bring our selues to nothing backe; and we
Do what we can, to do't so soone as hee.
With new diseases on our selues we warre,
And with new phisicke, a worse Engin farre.   160
Thus man, this worlds Vice-Emperor, in whom
All faculties, all graces are at home;
And if in other Creatures they appeare,
They're but mans ministers, and Legats there,
To worke on their rebellions, and reduce   165
Them to Ciuility, and to mans vse.
This man, whom God did wooe, and loth t'attend
Till man came vp, did downe to man descend,
This man, so great, that all that is, is his,
Oh what a trifle, and poore thing he is!   170
If man were any thing, he's nothing now:
Helpe, or at least some time to wast, allow
T'his other wants, yet when he did depart
With her, whom we lament, he lost his hart.
She, of whom th'Auncients seem'd to prophesie,   175
When they call'd vertues by the name of shee,
She in whom vertue was so much refin'd,
That for Allay vnto so pure a minde
Shee tooke the weaker Sex, she that could driue
The poysonous tincture, and the stayne of *Eue*,   180
Out of her thoughts, and deeds; and purifie
All, by a true religious Alchimy;
Shee, shee is dead; shee's dead: when thou knowest this,

---

153   close-weauing] *1633*; close-weaning *1611–25*

Thou knowest how poore a trifling thing man is.
And learn'st thus much by our Anatomee,   185
The heart being perish'd, no part can be free.
And that except thou feed (not banquet) on
The supernaturall food, Religion,
Thy better Grouth growes withered, and scant;
Be more then man, or thou'rt lesse then an Ant.   190
Then, as mankinde, so is the worlds whole frame
Quite out of ioynt, almost created lame:
For, before God had made vp all the rest,
Corruption entred, and deprau'd the best:
It seis'd the Angels, and then first of all   195
The world did in her Cradle take a fall,
And turn'd her braines, and tooke a generall maime
Wronging each ioynt of th'vniuersall frame.
The noblest part, man, felt it first; and than
Both beasts and plants, curst in the curse of man. *Decay of* 200
So did the world from the first houre decay,   *nature in*
The euening was beginning of the day,   *other parts.*
And now the Springs and Sommers which we see,
Like sonnes of women after fifty bee.
And new Philosophy cals all in doubt,   205
The Element of fire is quite put out;
The Sunne is lost, and th'earth, and no mans wit
Can well direct him, where to looke for it.
And freely men confesse, that this world's spent,
When in the Planets, and the Firmament   210
They seeke so many new; they see that this
Is crumbled out againe to his Atomis.
'Tis all in pieces, all cohaerence gone;
All iust supply, and all Relation:
Prince, Subiect, Father, Sonne, are things forgot,   215
For euery man alone thinkes he hath got

---

195   Angels,] *1612;* ~. *1611*

To be a Phoenix, and that there can bee
None of that kinde, of which he is, but hee.
This is the worlds condition now, and now
She that should all parts to reunion bow,   220
She that had all Magnetique force alone,
To draw, and fasten sundred parts in one;
She whom wise nature had inuented then
When she obseru'd that euery sort of men
Did in their voyage in this worlds Sea stray,   225
And needed a new compasse for their way;
Shee that was best, and first originall
Of all faire copies; and the generall
Steward to Fate; shee whose rich eyes, and brest,
Guilt the West Indies, and perfum'd the East;   230
Whose hauing breath'd in this world, did bestow
Spice on those Isles, and bad them still smell so,
And that rich Indie which doth gold interre,
Is but as single money, coyn'd from her:
She to whom this world must it selfe refer,   235
As Suburbs, or the Microcosme of her,
Shee, shee is dead; shee's dead: when thou knowst this,
Thou knowst how lame a cripple this world is.
And learnst thus much by our Anatomy,
That this worlds generall sickenesse doth not lie   240
In any humour, or one certaine part;
But, as thou sawest it rotten at the hart,
Thou seest a Hectique feuer hath got hold
Of the whole substance, not to be contrould,
And that thou hast but one way, not t'admit   245
The worlds infection, to be none of it.
For the worlds subtilst immateriall parts
Feele this consuming wound, and ages darts.

217   there] *1612 errata;* then *1611–69*
244   contrould,] *1633;* ~. *1611–25*

For the worlds beauty is decayd, or gone,
Beauty, that's colour, and proportion. *Disformity* 250
of parts.
We thinke the heauens enioy their Sphericall
Their round proportion embracing all.
But yet their various and perplexed course,
Obseru'd in diuers ages doth enforce
Men to finde out so many Eccentrique parts, 255
Such diuers downe-right lines, such ouerthwarts,
As disproportion that pure forme. It teares
The Firmament in eight and fortie sheeres,
And in those constellations there arise
New starres, and old do vanish from our eyes: 260
As though heau'n suffred earth-quakes, peace or war,
When new Townes rise, and olde demolish'd are.
They haue empayld within a Zodiake
The free-borne Sunne, and keepe twelue signes awake
To watch his steps; the Goat and Crabbe controule, 265
And fright him backe, who els to eyther Pole,
(Did not these Tropiques fetter him) might runne:
For his course is not round; nor can the Sunne
Perfit a Circle, or maintaine his way
One inche direct; but where he rose to day 270
He comes no more, but with a cousening line,
Steales by that point, and so is Serpentine:
And seeming weary with his reeling thus,
He meanes to sleepe, being now falne nearer vs.
So, of the stares which boast that they do runne 275
In Circle still, none ends where he begunne.
All their proportion's lame, it sinks, it swels.
For of Meridians, and Parallels,
Man hath weau'd out a net, and this net throwne

258 sheeres] *i.e.* shares
259 there] *1612 errata;* then *1611–69*
262 Townes] *1612 errata;* Towres *1611–69*
273 reeling] *1621;* recling *1611*

Vpon the Heauens, and now they are his owne.   280
Loth to goe vp the hill, or labor thus
To goe to heauen, we make heauen come to vs.
We spur, we raine the stars, and in their race
They're diuersly content t'obey our pace.
But keepes the earth her round proportion still?   285
Doth not a Tenarif, or higher Hill
Rise so high like a Rocke, that one might thinke
The floating Moone would shipwracke there, and sink?
Seas are so deepe, that Whales being strooke to day,
Perchance to morrow, scarse at middle way   290
Of their wish'd iourneys end, the bottom, dye.
And men, to sound depths, so much line vntie,
As one might iustly thinke, that there would rise
At end thereof, one of th'Antipodies:
If vnder all, a Vault infernall be,   295
(Which sure is spacious, except that we
Inuent another torment, that there must
Millions into a strait hote roome be thrust)
Then solidnes, and roundnes haue no place.
Are these but warts, and pock-holes in the face   300
Of th'earth? Thinke so: But yet confesse, in this
The worlds proportion disfigured is,
That those two legges whereon it doth relie,   *Disorder in the*
Reward and punishment are bent awrie.   *world.*
And, Oh, it can no more be questioned,   305
That beauties best, proportion, is dead,
Since euen griefe it selfe, which now alone
Is left vs, is without proportion.
Shee by whose lines proportion should bee
Examin'd, measure of all Symmetree,   310
Whom had that Ancient seen, who thought soules made
Of Harmony, he would at next haue said
That Harmony was shee, and thence infer,

That soules were but Resultances from her,
And did from her into our bodies go,   315
As to our eyes, the formes from obiects flow:
Shee, who if those great Doctors truely said
That th'Arke to mans proportions was made,
Had beene a type for that, as that might be
A type of her in this, that contrary   320
Both Elements, and Passions liu'd at peace
In her, who caus'd all Ciuill warre to cease.
Shee, after whom, what forme soe're we see,
Is discord, and rude incongruitee,
Shee, shee is dead, she's dead; when thou knowst this,   325
Thou knowst how vgly a monster this world is:
And learnst thus much by our Anatomee,
That here is nothing to enamor thee:
And that, not onely faults in inward parts,
Corruptions in our braines, or in our harts,   330
Poysoning the fountaines, whence our actions spring,
Endanger vs: but that if euery thing
Be not done fitly'nd in proportion,
To satisfie wise, and good lookers on,
(Since most men be such as most thinke they bee)   335
They're lothsome too, by this Deformitee.
For good, and well, must in our actions meete:
Wicked is not much worse then indiscreet.
But beauties other second Element,
Colour, and lustre now, is as neere spent.   340
And had the world his iust proportion,
Were it a ring still, yet the stone is gone.
As a compassionate Turcoyse which doth tell
By looking pale, the wearer is not well,
As gold fals sicke being stung with Mercury,   345
All the worlds parts of such complexion bee.
When nature was most busie, the first weeke,

Swadling the new-borne earth, God seemd to like,
That she should sport herselfe sometimes, and play,
To mingle, and vary colours euery day.   350
And then, as though she could not make inow,
Himselfe his various Rainbow did allow.
Sight is the noblest sense of any one,
Yet sight hath onely color to feed on,
And color is decayd: summers robe growes   355
Duskie, and like an oft dyed garment showes.
Our blushing redde, which vs'd in cheekes to spred,
Is inward sunke, and onely our soules are redde.
Perchance the world might haue recouered,
If she whom we lament had not beene dead: 360
But shee, in whom all white, and redde, and blue
(Beauties ingredients) voluntary grew,
As in an vnuext Paradise; from whom
Did all things verdure, and their lustre come,
Whose composition was miraculous,   365
Being all color, all Diaphanous,
(For Ayre, and Fire but thicke grosse bodies were,
And liueliest stones but drowsie, and pale to her,)
Shee, shee is dead; shee's dead: when thou knowst this,
Thou knowst how wan a Ghost this our world is: 370
And learnst thus much by our Anatomee,
That it should more affright, then pleasure thee.
And that, since all faire color then did sinke,
Tis now but wicked vanity to thinke,
To color vitious deeds with good pretence,   *Weaknesse*   375
Or with bought colors to illude mens sense.   *in the want of*
                                                  correspondence
Nor in ought more this worlds decay appeares,   *of heauen and*
Then that her influence the heau'n forbeares,   *earth*
Or that the Elements doe not feele this,
The father, or the mother barren is.   380
The clouds conceiue not raine, or doe not powre

In the due birth-time, downe the balmy showre.
Th'Ayre doth not motherly sit on the earth,
To hatch her seasons, and giue all things birth.
Spring-times were common cradles, but are toombes;   385
And false-conceptions fill the generall wombs.
Th'Ayre showes such Meteors, as none can see,
Not onely what they meane, but what they bee.
Earth such new wormes, as would haue troubled much,
Th'Egyptian Mages to haue made more such.   390
What Artist now dares boast that he can bring
Heauen hither, or constellate any thing,
So as the influence of those starres may bee
Imprisond in an Herbe, or Charme, or Tree,
And doe by touch, all which those starres could do?   395
The art is lost, and correspondence too.
For heauen giues little, and the earth takes lesse,
And man least knowes their trade, and purposes.
If this commerce twixt heauen and earth were not
Embarr'd, and all this trafique quite forgot,   400
Shee, for whose losse we haue lamented thus,
Would worke more fully'and pow'rfully on vs.
Since herbes, and roots by dying, lose not all,
But they, yea Ashes too, are medicinall,
Death could not quench her vertue so, but that   405
It would be (if not follow'd) wondred at:
And all the world would be one dying Swan,
To sing her funerall prayse, and vanish than.
But as some Serpents poison hurteth not,
Except it be from the liue Serpent shot,   410
So doth her vertue need her here, to fit
That vnto vs; she working more then it.
But she, in whom, to such maturity,
Vertue was growne, past growth, that it must die,
She from whose influence all Impressions came,   415

But, by Receiuers impotencies, lame,
Who, though she could not transubstantiate
All states to gold, yet guilded euery state,
So that some Princes haue some temperance;
Some Counsaylors some purpose to aduance   420
The common profite; and some people haue
Some stay, no more then Kings should giue, to craue;
Some women haue some taciturnity;
Some Nunneries, some graines of chastity.
She that did thus much, and much more could doe,   425
But that our age was Iron, and rusty too,
Shee, shee is dead; shee's dead: when thou knowst this,
Thou knowest how drie a Cinder this world is.
And learnst thus much by our Anatomy,
That 'tis in vaine to dew, or mollifie   430
It with thy Teares, or Sweat, or Bloud: no thing
Is worth our trauaile, griefe, or perishing,
But those rich ioyes, which did possesse her hart,
Of which shee's now partaker, and a part.
But as in cutting vp a man that's dead,   *Conclusion.*   435
The body will not last out to haue read
On euery part, and therefore men direct
Their speech to parts, that are of most effect;
So the worlds carcasse would not last, if I
Were punctuall in this Anatomy.   440
Nor smels it well to hearers, if one tell
Them their disease, who faine would think they're wel.
Here therefore be the end: And, blessed maid,
Of whom is meant what euer hath beene said,
Or shall be spoken well by any tongue,   445
Whose name refines course lines, and makes prose song,
Accept this tribute, and his first yeares rent,
Who till his darke short tapers end be spent,
As oft as thy feast sees this widowed earth,

Will yearely celebrate thy second birth,   450
That is, thy death. For though the soule of man
Be got when man is made, 'tis borne but than
When man doth die. Our body's as the wombe,
And as a mid-wife death directs it home.
And you her creatures, whom she workes vpon   455
And haue your last, and best concoction
From her example, and her vertue, if you
In reuerence to her, doe thinke it due,
That no one should her prayses thus reherse,
As matter fit for Chronicle, not verse,   460
Vouchsafe to call to minde, that God did make
A last, and lastingst peece, a song. He spake
To *Moses*, to deliuer vnto all,
That song: because he knew they would let fall,
The Law, the Prophets, and the History,   465
But keepe the song still in their memory.
Such an opinion (in due measure) made
Me this great Office boldly to inuade.
Nor could incomprehensiblenesse deterre
Me, from thus trying to emprison her.   470
Which when I saw that a strict graue could do,
I saw not why verse might not doe so too.
Verse hath a middle nature: heauen keepes soules,
The graue keeps bodies, verse the fame enroules.

---

474 fame] *1612 errata, 1633; same 1611–25*

A *Funerall Elegie.*

Tis lost, to trust a Tombe with such a ghest,
    Or to confine her in a Marble chest.
Alas, what's Marble, Ieat, or Porphiry,
    Priz'd with the Chrysolite of eyther eye,
Or with those Pearles, and Rubies which shee was?   5
    Ioyne the two Indies in one Tombe, 'tis glas;
And so is all to her materials,
    Though euery inche were ten escurials.
Yet shee's demolish'd: Can we keepe her then
    In workes of hands, or of the wits of men?   10
Can these memorials, ragges of paper, giue
    Life to that name, by which name they must liue?
Sickly, alas, short-liu'd, aborted bee
    Those Carkas verses, whose soule is not shee.
And can shee, who no longer would be shee,   15
    Being such a Tabernacle, stoope to bee
In paper wrap't; Or, when she would not lie
    In such a house, dwell in an Elegie?
But 'tis no matter; we may well allow
    Verse to liue so long as the world will now.   20
For her death wounded it. The world containes
    Princes for armes, and Counsailors for braines,

Lawyers for tongues, Diuines for hearts, and more,
    The Rich for stomachs, and for backes the Pore;
The Officers for hands, Merchants for feet   25
    By which remote and distant Countries meet.
But those fine spirits, which doe tune and set
    This Organ, are those peeces which beget
Wonder and loue; And these were shee; and shee
    Being spent, the world must needes decrepit bee.   30
For since death will proceed to triumph still,
    He can finde nothing, after her, to kill,
Except the world it selfe, so great as shee.
    Thus braue and confident may Nature bee,
Death cannot giue her such another blow,   35
    Because shee cannot such another show.
But must we say shee's dead? May't not be said
    That as a sundred Clocke is peece-meale laid,
Not to be lost, but by the makers hand
    Repolish'd, without error then to stand,   40
Or as the Affrique Niger streame enwombs
    It selfe into the earth, and after comes,
(Hauing first made a naturall bridge, to passe
    For many leagues,) farre greater then it was,
May't not be said, that her graue shall restore   45
    Her, greater, purer, firmer, then before?
Heauen may say this, and ioy in't; but can wee
    Who liue, and lacke her, here this vantage see?
What is't to vs, alas, if there haue beene
    An Angell made a Throne, or Cherubin?   50
We lose by't: And as aged men are glad
    Being tastlesse growne, to ioy in ioyes they had,
So now the sicke staru'd world must feed vpone
    This joy, that we had her, who now is gone.
Reioyce then nature, and this world, that you   55
    Fearing the last fires hastning to subdue

Your force and vigor, ere it were neere gone,
    Wisely bestow'd, and layd it all on one.
One, whose cleare body was so pure, and thin,
    Because it neede disguise no thought within.   60
T'was but a through-light scarfe, her minde t'enroule,
    Or exhalation breath'd out from her soule.
One, whom all men who durst no more, admir'd;
    And whom, who ere had worth enough, desir'd;
As when a Temple's built, Saints emulate   65
    To which of them, it shall be consecrate.
But as when Heau'n lookes on vs with new eyes,
    Those new starres eu'ry Artist exercise,
What place they should assigne to them they doubt,
    Argue, and agree not, till those starres go out: 70
So the world studied whose this peece should be,
    Till she can be no bodies else, nor shee:
But like a Lampe of Balsamum, desir'd
    Rather t'adorne, then last, shee soone expir'd;
Cloath'd in her Virgin white integrity;   75
    For mariage, though it doe not staine, doth dye.
To scape th'infirmities which waite vpone
    Woman, shee went away, before sh'was one.
And the worlds busie noyse to ouercome,
    Tooke so much death, as seru'd for *opium*.   80
For though she could not, nor could chuse to die,
    Shee'ath yeelded to too long an Extasie.
He which not knowing her sad History,
    Should come to reade the booke of destiny,
How faire and chast, humble and high shee'ad beene,   85
    Much promis'd, much perform'd, at not fifteene,
And measuring future things, by things before,
    Should turne the leafe to reade, and read no more,
Would thinke that eyther destiny mistooke,
    Or that some leafes were torne out of the booke.   90

But 'tis not so: Fate did but vsher her
    To yeares of Reasons vse, and then infer
Her destiny to her selfe; which liberty
    She tooke but for thus much, thus much to die.
Her modesty not suffering her to bee   95
    Fellow-Commissioner with destinee,
Shee did no more but die; if after her
    Any shall liue, which dare true good prefer,
Euery such person is her delegate,
    T'accomplish that which should haue beene her fate.   100
They shall make vp that booke, and shall haue thankes
    Of fate and her, for filling vp their blanks.
For future vertuous deeds are Legacies,
    Which from the gift of her example rise.
And 'tis in heau'n part of spirituall mirth,   105
    To see how well, the good play her, on earth.

FINIS.

THE SECOND ANNIUERSARIE.

OF

THE PROGRES

OF THE SOULE.

WHEREIN:

BY OCCASION OF THE

RELIGIOUS DEATH OF MISTRIS

ELIZABETH DRVRY

THE INCOMMODITIES OF THE SOULE

IN THIS LIFE AND HER EXALTATION IN

THE NEXT, ARE CONTEM-

PLATED.

•

The Harbinger
to the Progres.

Two soules moue here, and mine (a third) must moue
Paces of admiration, and of loue;
Thy soule (Deare Virgin) whose this tribute is,
Mou'd from this mortall sphere to liuely blisse;
And yet moues still, and still aspires to see   5
The worlds last day, thy glories full degree:
Like as those starres which thou ore-lookest farre,
Are in their place, and yet still moued are:
No soule (whiles with the lugage of this clay
It clogged is) can follow thee halfe way;   10
Or see thy flight; which doth our thoughts outgoe
So fast, that now the lightning moues but slow:
But now thou art as high in heauen flowne
As heau'ns from vs; what soule besides thine owne
Can tell thy ioyes, or say he can relate   15
Thy glorious Iournals in that blessed state?
I enuie thee (Rich soule) I enuy thee,
Although I cannot yet thy glory see:
And thou (Great spirit) which her's follow'd hast

8   are:] *1633;* ~ ∧ *1612–25*
15   relate] *1621;* re-relate *1612*

So fast, as none can follow thine so fast;   20
So farre as none can follow thine so farre,
(And if this flesh did not the passage barre
Had'st raught her) let me wonder at thy flight
Which long agone had'st lost the vulgar sight
And now mak'st proud the better eyes, that thay   25
Can see thee less'ned in thine aery way;
So while thou mak'st her soules Hy progresse knowne
Thou mak'st a noble progresse of thine owne,
From this worlds carcasse hauing mounted hie
To that pure life of Immortalitie;   30
Since thine aspiring thoughts themselues so raise
That more may not beseeme a creatures praise,
Yet still thou vow'st her more; and euery yeare
Mak'st a new progresse, while thou wandrest here;
Still vpwards mount; and let thy makers praise   35
Honor thy Laura, and adorne thy laies.
And since thy Muse her head in heauen shrouds
Oh let her neuer stoope below the clouds:
And if those glorious sainted soules may know
Or what we doe, or what we sing below,   40
Those acts, those songs shall still content them best
Which praise those awfull powers that make them blest.

---

27   soules Hy] *1612 errata, Davenport*; soules by *1612 text*
28   owne,] *1635*; ~. *1612–33*

The Second Anniuersary.

of
The Progres
of the Soule.

Nothing could make mee sooner to confesse   *The entrance.*
That this world had an euerlastingnesse,
Then to consider, that a yeare is runne,
Since both this lower worlds, and the Sunnes Sunne,
The Lustre, and the vigor of this All,   5
Did set; t'were Blasphemy, to say, did fall.
But as a ship which hath strooke saile, doth runne,
By force of that force which before, it wonne,
Or as sometimes in a beheaded man,
Though at those two Red seas, which freely ran,   10
One from the Trunke, another from the Head,
His soule be saild, to her eternall bed,
His eies will twinckle, and his tongue will roll,
As though he beckned, and cal'd backe his Soul,
He graspes his hands, and he puls vp his feet,   15
And seemes to reach, and to step forth to meet

1   confesse∧] *1633;* ~. *1612–25*
10   Though] *1612 errata, 1633;* Through *1612–25*
16   meet∧] *1621;* ~. *1612*

His soule; when all these motions which we saw,
Are but as Ice, which crackles at a thaw:
Or as a Lute, which in moist weather, rings
Her knell alone, by cracking at her strings.   20
So strugles this dead world, now shee is gone;
For there is motion in corruption.
As some Daies are, at the Creation nam'd,
Before the sunne, the which fram'd Daies, was fram'd,
So after this sunnes set, some show appeares,   25
And orderly vicisitude of yeares.
Yet a new Deluge, and of Lethe flood,
Hath drown' vs all, All haue forgot all good,
Forgetting her, the maine Reserue of all;
Yet in this Deluge, grosse and generall,   30
Thou seest mee striue for life; my life shalbe,
To bee hereafter prais'd, for praysing thee,
Immortal Mayd, who though thou wouldst refuse
The name of Mother, be vnto my Muse,
A Father since her chast Ambition is,   35
Yearely to bring forth such a child as this.
These Hymes may worke on future wits, and so
May great Grand-children of thy praises grow.
And so, though not Reuiue, enbalme, and spice
The world, which else would putrify with vice.   40
For thus, Man may extend thy progeny,
Vntill man doe but vanish, and not die.
These Hymns thy issue, may encrease so long,
As till Gods great Venite change the song.
Thirst for that time, O my insatiate soule,   *A iust*   45
And serue thy thirst, with Gods safe-sealing Bowle.   *disestimation*
Bee thirsty still, and drinke still till thou goe;   *of this world.*

17   soule;] *1621; ~, 1612*
29   all;] *1635; ~, 1612–33*
41   For] *1621; for 1612*
46   safe-sealing] *1649; safe-fealing 1612–39*
47   till∧] *1612 errata, 1621; ~, 1612 text*

'Tis th'onely Health, to be Hydropique so.
Forget this rotten world; And vnto thee,
Let thine owne times as an old story be,   50
Be not concern'd: study not why, nor whan;
Do not so much, as not beleeue a man.
For though to erre, be worst, to try truths forth,
Is far more busines, then this world is worth.
The World is but a Carkas; thou art fed   55
By it, but as a worme, that carcas bred;
And why shouldst thou, poore worme, consider more,
When this world will grow better then before,
Then those thy fellow-wormes doe thinke vpone
That carkasses last resurrectione.   60
Forget this world, and scarse thinke of it so,
As of old cloaths, cast of a yeare agoe.
To be thus stupid is Alacrity;
Men thus lethargique haue best Memory.
Looke vpward; that's towards her, whose happy state   65
We now lament not, but congratulate.
Shee, to whom all this world was but a stage,
Where all sat harkning how her youthfull age
Should be emploid, because in all, shee did,
Some Figure of the Golden times, was hid.   70
Who could not lacke, what ere this world could giue,
Because shee was the forme, that made it liue;
Nor could complaine, that this world was vnfit,
To be staid in, then when shee was in it;
Shee that first tried indifferent desires   75
By vertue, and vertue by religious fires,
Shee to whose person Paradise adhear'd,
As Courts to Princes; shee whose eies enspheard

---

48 'Tis] *1612 errata;* T'o *1612 text*
48 Hydropique] *1612 errata;* Hydroptique *1612–69*
50 be,] *1639;* ~ ∧ *1612–35*
67 was] *1612 errata, 1633;* twas *1612–25*

Star-light inough, t'haue made the South controll,
(Had shee beene there) the Star-full Northern Pole,   80
Shee, shee is gone; shee is gone; when thou knowest this,
What fragmentary rubbidge this world is
Thou knowest, and that it is not worth a thought;
He honors it too much that thinks it nought.
Thinke then, My soule, that death is but a Groome,   *Contemplation*
Which brings a Taper to the outward roome,   *of our*
                                                        state in
Whence thou spiest first a little glimmering light,   *our death-*
And after brings it nearer to thy sight: *bed.*
For such approches doth Heauen make in death.
Thinke thy selfe laboring now with broken breath,   90
And thinke those broken and soft Notes to bee
Diuision, and thy happiest Harmonee.
Thinke thee laid on thy death bed, loose and slacke;
And thinke that but vnbinding of a packe,
To take one precious thing, thy soule, from thence.   95
Thinke thy selfe parch'd with feuers violence,
Anger thine Ague more, by calling it
Thy Physicke; chide the slacknesse of the fit.
Thinke that thou hearst thy knell, and thinke no more,
But that, as Bels cal'd thee to Church before,   100
So this, to the Triumphant Church, cals thee.
Thinke Satans Sergeants round about thee bee,
And thinke that but for Legacies they thrust;
Giue one thy Pride, to'another giue thy Lust:
Giue them those sinnes which they gaue thee before,   105
And trust th'immaculate blood to wash thy score.
Thinke thy frinds weeping round, and thinke that thay
Weepe but because they goe not yet thy way.
Thinke that they close thine eyes, and thinke in this,
That they confesse much in the world, amisse,   110

82   is∧] *1633;* ∼. *1612–25*
86   roome] *1621;* romme *1612*

Who dare not trust a dead mans eye with that,
Which they from God, and Angels couer not.
Thinke that they shroud thee vp, and thinke from thence
They reinuest thee in white innocence.
Thinke that thy body rots, and (if so lowe,   115
Thy soule exalted so, thy thoughts can goe,)
Thinke the a Prince, who of themselues create
Wormes which insensibly deuoure their state.
Thinke that they bury thee, and thinke that rite
Laies thee to sleepe but a saint Lucies night.   120
Thinke these things cheerefully: and if thou bee
Drowsie or slacke, remember then that shee,
Shee whose Complexion was so euen made,
That which of her Ingredients should inuade
The other three, no Feare, no Art could guesse: 125
So far were all remou'd from more or lesse.
But as in Mithridate, or iust perfumes,
Where all good things being met, no one presumes
To gouerne, or to triumph on the rest,
Onely because all were, no part was best.   130
And as, though all doe know, that quantities
Are made of lines, and lines from Points arise,
None can these lines or quantities vnioynt,
And say this is a line, or this a point,
So though the Elements and Humors were   135
In her, one could not say, this gouernes there.
Whose euen constitution might haue wonne
Any disease to venter on the Sunne,
Rather then her: and make a spirit feare
That he to disuniting subiect were.   140
To whose proportions if we would compare

---

116   goe,] *1625;* ~. *1612–21*
119   rite] *1612 errata;* right *1612–69*
129   on] *1621;* no *1612*
137   wonne] *1612 errata, 1633;* worne *1612–25*

Cubes, th'are vnstable; Circles, Angulare;
Shee who was such a Chaine, as Fate emploies
To bring mankind, all Fortunes it enioies,
So fast, so euen wrought, as one would thinke,   145
No Accident, could threaten any linke,
Shee, shee embrac'd a sicknesse, gaue it meat,
The purest Blood, and Breath, that ere it eat.
And hath taught vs that though a good man hath
Title to Heauen, and plead it by his Faith,   150
And though he may pretend a conquest, since
Heauen was content to suffer violence,
Yea though he plead a long possession too,
(For they'are in Heauen on Earth, who Heauens workes do,)
Though he had right, and power, and Place before,   155
Yet Death must vsher, and vnlocke the doore.
Thinke further on thy selfe, my soule, and thinke;   *Incommodi-*
How thou at first wast made but in a sinke;   *ties of*
Thinke that it argued some infermitee,   *the Soule*
That those two soules, which then thou foundst in mee, *in the Body.* 160
Thou fedst vpon, and drewst into thee, both
My second soule of sence, and first of growth.
Thinke but how poore thou wast, how obnoxious,
Whom a small lump of flesh could poison thus.
This curded milke, this poore vnlittered whelpe   165
My body, could, beyond escape, or helpe,
Infect thee with originall sinne, and thou
Couldst neither then refuse, nor leaue it now.
Thinke that no stubborne sullen Anchorit,
Which fixt to'a Pillar, or a Graue doth sit   170
Bedded and Bath'd in all his Ordures, dwels
So fowly as our soules, in their first-built Cels.
Thinke in how poore a prison thou didst lie

---

153   a long] *1621;* along *1612*
161   and] *1621;* And *1612*
171   Bedded] *1621;* Beddded *1612*

After, enabled but to sucke, and crie.
Thinke, when t'was growne to most, t'was a poore Inne,   175
A Prouince Pack'd vp in two yards of skinne,
And that vsurped, or threatned with the rage
Of sicknesses, or their true mother, Age.
But thinke that Death hath now enfranchis'd thee,   *Her liberty*
Thou hast thy'expansion now and libertee;   *by death.*
Thinke that a rusty Peece, discharg'd, is flowen
In peeces, and the bullet is his owne,
And freely flies: This to thy soule allow,
Thinke thy sheell broke, thinke thy Soule hatch'd but now.
And thinke this slow-pac'd soule, which late did cleaue,   185
To'a body, and went but by the bodies leaue,
Twenty, perchance, or thirty mile a day,
Dispatches in a minute all the way,
Twixt Heauen, and Earth: shee staies not in the Ayre,
To looke what Meteors there themselues prepare;   190
Shee carries no desire to know, nor sense,
Whether th'Ayrs middle Region be intense,
For th'Element of fire, shee doth not know,
Whether shee past by such a place or no;
Shee baits not at the Moone, nor cares to trie,   195
Whether in that new world, men liue, and die.
Venus retards her not, to'enquire, how shee
Can, (being one Star) Hesper, and Vesper bee;
Hee that charm'd Argus eies, sweet Mercury,
Workes not on her, who now is growen all Ey;   200
Who, if shee meete the body of the Sunne,
Goes through, not staying till his course be runne;
Who finds in Mars his Campe, no corps of Guard;

---

176   skinne,] *1633;* ~. *1612–25*
180   expansion] *1612 errata, 1625;* expausion *1612–21*
184   sheell] *i.e.* shell
197   retards] *1612 errata, 1633;* recards *1612–25*
198   bee;] *1633;* ~, *1612–25*

Nor is by Ioue, nor by his father bard;
But ere shee can consider how shee went,   205
At once is at, and through the Firmament.
And as these stars were but so many beades
Strunge on one string, speed vndistinguish'd leades
Her through those spheares, as through the beades, a string,
Whose quicke succession makes it still one thing: 210
As doth the Pith, which, least our Bodies slacke,
Strings fast the little bones of necke, and backe;
So by the soule doth death string Heauen and Earth,
For when our soule enioyes this her third birth,
(Creation gaue her one, a second, grace,)   215
Heauen is as neare, and present to her face,
As colours are, and obiects, in a roome
Where darknesse was before, when Tapers come.
This must, my soule, thy long-short Progresse bee;
To'aduance these thoughts, remember then, that shee   220
Shee, whose faire body no such prison was,
But that a soule might well be pleas'd to passe
An Age in her; shee whose rich beauty lent
Mintage to others beauties, for they went
But for so much, as they were like to her;   225
Shee, in whose body (if wee dare prefer
This low world, to so high a mark, as shee,)
The Westerne treasure, Esterne spiceree,
Europe, and Afrique, and the vnknowen rest
Were easily found, or what in them was best;   230
And when w'haue made this large Discoueree,
Of all in her some one part there will bee
Twenty such parts, whose plenty and riches is
Inough to make twenty such worlds as this;
Shee, whom had they knowne, who did first betroth   235
The Tutelar Angels, and assigned one, both

---

232   there] *1612 errata*; then *1612–69*

To Nations, Cities, and to Companies,
To Functions, Offices, and Dignities,
And to each seuerall man, to him, and him,
They would haue giuen her one for euery limme;   240
Shee, of whose soule, if we may say, t'was Gold,
Her body was th'Electrum, and did hold
Many degrees of that; we vnderstood
Her by her sight, her pure and eloquent blood
Spoke in her cheekes, and so distinckly wrought,   245
That one might almost say, her bodie thought,
Shee, shee, thus richly, and largely hous'd, is gone:
And chides vs slow-pac'd snailes, who crawle vpon
Our prisons prison, earth, nor thinke vs well
Longer, then whil'st we beare our brittle shell.   250
But t'were but little to haue chang'd our roome,
If, as we were in this our liuing Tombe
Oppress'd with ignorance, we still were so.
Poore soule in this thy flesh what do'st thou know.
Thou know'st thy selfe so little, as thou know'st not,
How thou did'st die, nor how thou wast begot.
Thou neither knowst, how thou at first camest in,
Nor how thou took'st the poyson of mans sin.
Nor dost thou, (though thou knowst, that thou art so)
By what way thou art made immortall, know.   260
Thou art to narrow, wretch, to comprehend
Euen thy selfe: yea though thou wouldst but bend
To know thy body. Haue not all soules thought
For many ages, that our body'is wrought
Of Ayre, and Fire, and other Elements?   265
And now they thinke of new ingredients.
And one soule thinkes one, and another way
Another thinkes, and ty's an euen lay.

Her igno-
rance in
this life
and knowl-
edge in
the next.

243   ∧we] *1635;* (∼ *1612–33*
253   so.] *1625;* ∼, *1612–21*
268   lay.] *1621;* ∼ ∧*1612*

Knowst thou but how the stone doth enter in
The bladders Caue, and neuer breake the skin?   270
Knowst thou how blood, which to the hart doth flow,
Doth from one ventricle to th'other go?
And for the putrid stuffe, which thou dost spit,
Knowst thou how thy lungs haue attracted it?
There are no passages so that there is   275
(For ought thou knowst) piercing of substances.
And of those many opinions which men raise
Of Nailes and Haires, dost thou know which to praise?
What hope haue we to know our selues, when wee
Know not the least things, which for our vse bee?   280
We see in Authors, too stiffe to recant,
A hundred controuersies of an Ant.
And yet one watches, starues, freeses, and sweats,
To know but Catechismes and Alphabets
Of vnconcerning things, matters of fact;   285
How others on our stage their parts did Act;
What Caesar did, yea, and what Cicero said.
Why grasse is greene, or why our blood is red,
Are mysteries which none haue reach'd vnto.
In this low forme, poore soule what wilt thou doe?   290
When wilt thou shake off this Pedantery,
Of being taught by sense, and Fantasy?
Thou look'st through spectacles; small things seeme great,
Below; But vp vnto the watch-towre get,
And see all things despoyld of fallacies: 295
Thou shalt not peepe through lattices of eies,
Nor heare through Laberinths of eares, nor learne
By circuit, or collections to discerne.
In Heauen thou straight know'st all, concerning it,
And what concerns it not, shall straight forget.   300

---

281   recant,] *1633; ∼. 1612–25*
292   taught] *1612 errata, 1633; thought 1612–25*

There thou (but in no other schoole) maist bee
Perchance, as learned, and as full, as shee,
Shee who all Libraries had throughly red
At home, in her owne thoughts, and practised
So much good as would make as many more: 305
Shee whose example they must all implore,
Who would or doe, or thinke well, and confesse
That aie the vertuous Actions they expresse,
Are but a new, and worse edition,
Of her some one thought, or one action: 310
Shee, who in th'Art of knowing Heauen, was growen
Here vpon Earth, to such perfection,
That shee hath, euer since to Heauen shee came,
(In a far fairer print,) but read the same:
Shee, shee, not satisfied with all this waite,   315
(For so much knowledge, as would ouer-fraite
Another, did but Ballast her) is gone,
As well t'enioy, as get perfectione.
And cals vs after her, in that shee tooke,
(Taking herselfe) our best, and worthiest booke.   320
Returne not, my soule, from this extasee,   *Of our company*
And meditation of what thou shalt bee,   *in this life*
To earthly thoughts, till it to thee appeare,   *and in the*
With whom thy conuersation must be there.   *next.*
With whom wilt thou Conuerse? what station   325
Canst thou choose out, free from infection,
That wil nor giue thee theirs, nor drinke in thine?
Shalt thou not finde a spungy slack Diuine
Drinke and sucke in th'Instructions of Great men,
And for the word of God, vent them agen?   330
Are there not some Courts, (And then, no things bee

---

304   and] *1621*; And *1612*
308   aie] *i.e.* aye
314   print] *1612 errata, 1635*; point *1612–33*

So like as Courts) which, in this let vs see,
That wits and tongues of Libellars are weake,
Because they doe more ill, then these can speake?
The poyson'is gone through all, poysons affect   335
Chiefly the cheefest parts, but some effect
In Nailes, and Haires, yea excrements, will show;
So will the poyson of sinne, in the most low.
Vp vp, my drowsie soule, where thy new eare
Shall in the Angels songs no discord heare;   340
Where thou shalt see the blessed Mother-maid
Ioy in not being that, which men haue said.
Where shee'is exalted more for being good,
Then for her interest, of mother-hood.
Vp to those Patriarckes, which did longer sit   345
Expecting Christ, then they'haue enioy'd him yet.
Vp to those Prophets, which now gladly see
Their Prophecies growen to be Historee.
Vp to th'Apostles, who did brauely runne,
All the Sunnes course, with more light then the Sunne.   350
Vp to those Martyrs, who did calmely bleed
Oyle to th'Apostles lamps, dew to their seed.
Vp to those Virgins, who thought that almost
They made ioyntenants with the Holy Ghost,
If they to any should his Temple giue.   355
Vp, vp, for in that squadron there doth liue
Shee, who hath carried thether, new degrees
(As to their number) to their dignitees.
Shee, who beeing to herselfe a state, enioyd
All royalties which any state emploid,   360
For shee made wars, and triumph'd; reson still
Did not ouerthrow, but rectifie her will:

---

338   will] *1612 errata;* wise *1612–25*
353   thought] *1612 errata, 1633;* thoughts *1612–25*
359   herselfe∧ . . . state,] *1633;* ~, . . . ~ ∧*1612–25*
361   triumph'd;] *1633;* ~, *1612–25*

And shee made peace, for no peace is like this,
That beauty and chastity together kisse:
Shee did high iustice; for shee crucified   365
Euery first motion of rebellious pride:
And shee gaue pardons, and was liberall,
For, onely herselfe except, shee pardond all:
Shee coynd, in this, that her impressions gaue
To all our actions all the worth they haue: 370
Shee gaue protections; the thoughts of her brest
Satans rude Officers could nere arrest.
As these prerogatiues being met in one,
Made her a soueraigne state, religion
Made her a Church; and these two made her all.   375
Shee who was all this All, and could not fall
To worse, by company; (for shee was still
More Antidote, then all the world was ill,)
Shee, shee doth leaue it, and by Death, suruiue
All this, in Heauen; whither who doth not striue   380
The more, because shee'is there, he doth not know
That accidentall ioyes in Heauen doe grow.
But pause, My soule, and study ere thou fall   *Of essentiall*
On accidentall ioyes, th'essentiall.   *ioy in this*
Still before Accessories doe abide   *life and in*
A triall, must the principall be tride.   *the next.*
And what essentiall ioy canst thou expect
Here vpon earth? what permanent effect
Of transitory causes? Dost thou loue
Beauty? (And Beauty worthyest is to moue)   390
Poore couse'ned cose'nor, that she, and that thou,
Which did begin to loue, are neither now.
You are both fluid, chang'd since yesterday;
Next day repaires, (but ill) last daies decay.

---

378   ill)] *1635;* ~ ∧ *1612–33*
380   whither] *1612 errata, 1635;* whether *1612–33*

Nor are, (Although the riuer keep the name)   395
Yesterdaies waters, and to daies the same.
So flowes her face, and thine eies, neither now
That saint, nor Pilgrime, which your louing vow
Concernd, remaines; but whil'st you thinke you bee
Constant, you'are howrely in inconstancee.   400
Honour may haue pretence vnto our loue,
Because that God did liue so long aboue
Without this Honour, and then lou'd it so,
That he at last made Creatures to bestow
Honor on him; not that he needed it,   405
But that, to his hands, man might grow more fit.
But since all honors from inferiors flow,
(For they doe giue it; Princes doe but show
Whom they would haue so honord) and that this
On such opinions, and capacities   410
Is built, as rise, and fall, to more and lesse,
Alas, tis but a casuall happinesse.
Hath euer any man to'himselfe assigned
This or that happinesse, to'arrest his minde,
But that another man, which takes a worse,   415
Thinks him a foole for hauing tane that course?
They who did labour Babels tower t'erect,
Might haue considerd, that for that effect,
All this whole solid Earth could not allow
Nor furnish forth Materials enow;   420
And that this Center, to raise such a place
Was far to little, to haue beene the Base;
No more affoords this world, foundatione
To erect true ioye, were all the meanes in one.

---

398   vow] *1612 errata, 1633;* row *1612–25*
404   to] *1621;* to to *1612*
416   Thinks] *1633;* Thinke *1612–25*
417   t'erect] *1612 errata;* to'rect *1612 text*
423   world] *1633;* worlds *1612–25*

But as the Heathen made them seuerall gods,   425
Of all Gods Benefits, and all his Rods,
(For as the Wine, and Corne, and Onions are
Gods vnto them, so Agues bee, and war)
And as by changing that whole precious Gold
To such small copper coynes, they lost the old,   430
And lost their onely God, who euer must
Be sought alone, and not in such a thrust,
So much mankind true happinesse mistakes;
No Ioye enioyes that man, that many makes.
Then, soule, to thy first pitch worke vp againe;   435
Know that all lines which circles doe containe,
For once that they the center touch, do touch
Twice the circumference; and be thou such.
Double on Heauen, thy thoughts on Earth emploid;
All will not serue; Onely who haue enioyd   440
The sight of God, in fulnesse, can thinke it;
For it is both the obiect, and the wit.
This is essentiall ioye, where neither hee
Can suffer Diminution, nor wee;
Tis such a full, and such a filling good;   445
Had th'Angels once look'd on him, they had stood.
To fill the place of one of them, or more,
Shee whom we celebrate, is gone before.
Shee, who had Here so much essentiall ioye,
As no chance could distract, much lesse destroy;   450
Who with Gods presence was acquainted so,
(Hearing, and speaking to him) as to know
His face, in any naturall Stone, or Tree,
Better then when in Images they bee:
Who kept, by diligent deuotion,   455
Gods Image, in such reparation,

---

435   vp] *1633*; vpon *1612–25*
449   ioye,] *1633*; ~. *1612–25*

Within her heart, that what decay was growen,
Was her first Parents fault, and not her own:
Who being solicited to any Act,
Still heard God pleading his safe precontract;   460
Who by a faithfull confidence, was here
Betrothed to God, and now is married there,
Whose twilights were more cleare, then our mid day,
Who dreamt deuoutlier, then most vse to pray;
Who being heare fild with grace, yet stroue to bee,   465
Both where more grace, and more capacitee
At once is giuen: shee to Heauen is gone,
Who made this world in some proportion
A heauen, and here, became vnto vs all,
Ioye, (as our ioyes admit) essentiall.   470
But could this low world ioyes essentiall touch,   *Of acciden-*
Heauens accidentall ioyes would passe them much.   *tall ioyes*
How poore and lame, must then our casuall bee?   *in both*
If thy Prince will his subiects to call thee   *places.*
My Lord, and this doe swell thee, thou art than,   475
By being a greater, growen to be lesse Man.
When no Physician of Redresse can speake,
A ioyfull casuall violence may breake
A dangerous Apostem in thy brest;
And whilst thou ioyest in this, the dangerous rest,   480
The bag may rise vp, and so strangle thee.
What eie was casuall, may euer bee.
What should the Nature change? Or make the same
Certaine, which was but casuall, when it came?
All casuall ioye doth loud and plainly say,   485
Onely by comming, that it can away.
Onely in Heauen ioies strength is neuer spent;
And accidentall things are permanent.

---

476   Man.] *1633;* ∼, *1612–25*
477   Redresse] *1612 errata, 1633;* Reders *1612–25*
482   eie] *i.e.* aye

Ioy of a soules arriuall neere decaies;
For that soule euer ioyes, and euer staies.   490
Ioy that their last great Consummation
Approches in the resurrection;
When earthly bodies more celestiall
Shalbe, then Angels were, for they could fall;
This kind of ioy doth euery day admit   495
Degrees of grouth, but none of loosing it.
In this fresh ioy, tis no small part, that shee,
Shee, in whose goodnesse, he that names degree,
Doth iniure her; (Tis losse to be cald best,
There where the stuffe is not such as the rest)   500
Shee, who left such a body, as euen shee
Onely in Heauen could learne, how it can bee
Made better; for shee rather was two soules,
Or like to full, on both sides written Rols,
Where eies might read vpon the outward skin,   505
As strong Records for God, as mindes within.
Shee, who by making full perfection grow,
Peeces a Circle, and still keepes it so,
Long'd for, and longing for'it, to heauen is gone,
Where shee receiues, and giues addition.   510
Here in a place, where mis-deuotion frames   *Conclusion.*
A thousand praiers to saints, whose very names
The ancient Church knew not, Heauen knowes not yet,
And where, what lawes of poetry admit,
Lawes of religion, haue at least the same,   515
Immortall Maid, I might inuoque thy name.
Could any Saint prouoke that appetite,
Thou here shouldst make mee a french conuertite.
But thou wouldst not; nor wouldst thou be content,
To take this, for my second yeeres true Rent,   520

---

506   within.] *1649; ~, 1612–39*
516   inuoque] *1612 errata, 1633; iuoque 1612–25*

Did this Coine beare any other stampe, then his,
That gaue thee power to doe, me, to say this.
Since his will is, that to posteritee,
Thou shouldest for life, and death, a patterne bee,
And that the world should notice haue of this,   525
The purpose, and th' Autority is his;
Thou art the Proclamation; and I ame
The Trumpet, at whose voice the people came.

---

522   doe,] *1612 errata, 1633;* ∼ ∧ *1612–25*

FINIS.

Historical Collation

[The following is the result of a collation of at least two copies of all the editions of the *Anniversaries* in the seventeenth century: those of 1611, 1612, 1621, 1625, 1633, 1635, 1639, 1649, 1650, and 1669. The lemmata are taken from the present text; the sigla after the square brackets represent substantive or, in a few borderline cases, semi-substantive variants. The only exceptions are the corrections from the 1612 errata slip, which are reprinted in their entirety. All editions for which sigla are not given for a particular variant may be assumed to agree with the present text.]

Title The First Anniuersarie.]
        om. 1611

Title An] *om. 1635–69*

Praise of the Dead

8	While] Whiles *1639–69*	43	an . . . songs] *om.* . . .
21	is vs] it is *1669*		songs *1621–25; om.* . . .
34	where] were *1612–25*		of songs *1633–69*
36	in] and *1633–69*	45	whose] whole *1649–69*
39	tongue] tongues *1649–69*	47	our] *om. 1669*

First Anniversary

Title The First Anniuersary.]
        om. 1611

1 *Marginal note   The entrie into the worke.]   om. 1611, 1625–69. 1611, 1635–69 print no marginal notes*

2   Whom] Who *1633*
2   they celebrate] doe celebrate
     1621–69
14   then] them *1649–69*
40   times] time *1635–69*
50   glue] give *1649–69*
66   *Marginal note   What*
     life the world hath still]
     om. 1625–33
79   though] thought *1621–33*
88   *Marginal note   sick-*
     nesses] *sicknesse 1621–33*
88   *Marginal note   world*]
     Word 1625
89   then] them *1649–69*
130 new] *1611, 1612 errata;*
     true 1612–69
135 man∧] ~. *1612–25*; ~,
     1633–69
144 scarse] *1612 errata, 1625–*
     69; scarsc *1611*; searse
     1612–21
153 close-weauing] close-wean-
     ing *1611–25*
161 Thus] This *1635–69*

164 there] thers *1621–25*
181 thoughts] thought *1621–33*
186 no] no no *1621*
217 there] *1612 errata;* then
     1611–69
258 sheeres] sheires *1633–35;*
     shieres *1639–69*
259 those] these *1612–69*
259 there] *1612 errata;* then
     1611–69
262 Townes] *1612 errata;*
     Towres *1611–69*
273 with] of *1635–69*
284 pace] *1611, 1612 errata,*
     1635–69; peace *1612–33*
286 Tenarif] Tenarus *1633–69*
318 proportions] proportion
     1621–69
394 an] a *1635–69*
415 Impressions] Impression
     1612–69
442 they're] thy're *1633*
474 fame] *1612 errata, 1633–*
     69; same *1611–25*

Funerall Elegie

Title A Funerall Elegie.] The
       Funerall Elegie vppon the
       death of Mrs Elizabeth
       Drury. *B*
1   lost] losse *1635–69*
13   aborted] Abortive *1635–69*
18   a] an *1635–69*
18   an] a *B*

33   as] *om. 1625;* was *1633–69*
48   her, here∧] ~, ~, *1633;*
     ~ ∧ ~, *1635–69*
64   worth] worke *1633*
76   doe] doth *1633–69, B*
83   sad] said *1612–33, B*
FINIS.] *om. 1633–69;* J.D. *B*

Harbinger to the Progres

4   from] form *1649–50*
12 that] as *1635–69*
15 relate] re-relate *1612*
23 raught] caught *1621–69*
27 soules Hy] *1612 errata,*
     Davenport; soules by
     1612 text; soule by *1621–*
     69
34 while] whilst *1669*
35 vpwards] vpward *1621–69*

Second Anniversary

1   *Marginal note   The en-*
     trance.] om. *1625–33*
10 Though] *1612 errata, 1633–*
     69; Through *1612–25*
12 be] he *1621–33*
13 twinckle] twincke *1625*
42 vanish] banish *1625*
43 thy] they *1621–25*
45 *Marginal note   disesti-*
     mation] estimation
     1625–33
46 safe-sealing] safe-fealing
     1612–39
47 till∧] *1612 errata, 1621–*
     69; ∼, *1612 text*
48 'Tis] *1612 errata;* T'o *1612*
     text; To *1621–69*
48 Hydropique] *1612 errata;*
     Hydroptique *1612–69*
51 nor] or *1669*
67 was] *1612 errata, 1633–69;*
     twas *1612–25*
96 parch'd] pach'd *1625;*
     patch'd *1633–35*
103 thrust] trust *1669*
119 rite] *1612 errata;* right
     1612–69

129 on] no *1612*
137 wonne] *1612 errata, 1633–*
     69; worne *1612–25*
153 a long] along *1612*
154 who] whose *1669*
157 *Marginal note   Incom-*
     modities of the Soule in
     the Body.] om. *1625–33*
173 didst] dost *1669*
177 the] a *1633–69*
180 expansion] *1612 errata,*
     1625–69; expausion
     1612–21
197 retards] *1612 errata, 1633–*
     69; recards *1612–25*
209 the] those *1669*
214 this] om. *1649–69*
216 as] om. *1669*
219–220 be; . . . thoughts,]
     ∼, . . . ∼; *1633–69*
224 others] other *1633–69*
232 there] *1612 errata;* then
     1612–69
234 make] wake *1635–39*
243 vnderstood] vnstood *1621–*
     25
251 *Marginal note   Her ig-*

norance in this life and
knowledge in the next.]
om. 1633

266   new] knew *1635–39*
287   said.] ~, *1633–69*
292   taught] *1612 errata, 1633–*
        69; thought *1612–25*
300   shall] shalt *1633–50*
308   aie] are *1625;* all *1633–69*
314   print] *1612 errata, 1635–*
        69; point *1612–33*
315   not] nor *1669*
323   earthly] early *1625*
327   nor . . . nor] not . . .
        nor *1625–69*
338   will] *1612 errata;* wise
        1612–25; lyes *1633–69*
353   thought] *1612 errata, 1633–*
        69; thoughts *1612–25*
366   rebellious] rebellions *1635–*
        69
369   impressions] impression
        1633–69
380   whither] *1612 errata, 1635–*
        69; whether *1612–33*
398   vow] *1612 errata, 1633–69;*

        row *1612–25*
402   that] *that 1633*
404   to] to to *1612*
416   Thinks] Thinke *1612–25*
417   t'erect] *1612 errata;* to'rect
        1612 text; to'erect *1621–*
        69
421   this] his *1621–69*
423   world] worlds *1612–25*
429   that] the *1625*
435   vp] vpon *1612–25*
475   swell] smell *1669*
476   a] *om. 1625–69*
477   Redresse] *1612 errata,*
        1633–69; Reders *1612–*
        25
482   eie] eye *1621–25;* e'r *1633–*
        69
501   euen] euer *1625*
504   full,] ~ ∧ *1633–69*
516   inuoque] *1612 errata, 1633–*
        69; inroque *1612–25*
522   doe,] *1612 errata, 1633–69;*
        ~ ∧ *1612–25*
FINIS.] *om. 1633–69*

Press Variants

[Copies collated: CSmH (The Henry E. Huntington Library) and K (G. L. Keynes).]

SHEET A (*outer form*)

Corrected: K
Uncorrected: CSmH

Sig.A7.
117   slow-pac'd] slow pac'd

SHEET A (*inner form*)

Corrected: CSmH
Uncorrected: K

Sig.A7^v.
133   euery] enery

SHEET B (*inner form*)

Corrected: CSmH
Uncorrected: K

113

Sig.B1ᵛ.
  237   this,] this

SHEET B *(outer form)*

Corrected: K
Uncorrected: CSmH

Sig.B4ᵛ.
  385   toombes;] toombes

PRESS VARIANTS IN *THE SECOND ANNIVERSARY* (1612)

[Copies collated: DFo (The Folger Shakespeare Library), MH (Harvard), CtY¹ (Yale, Thorn-Drury; wants C1, C8, D1, D8, G3, H3), CtY² (Yale, Rosenbloom; wants D2–7), CSmH (The Henry E. Huntington Library), and K (G. L. Keynes).]

Variants noted: none.

Abbreviations

Unless otherwise noted references to Donne's poetry are to Sir Herbert J. C. Grierson's *Poems of John Donne* (Oxford, 1912), 2 vols. References to the prose work are to the following editions:

Biathanatos
Biathanatos, introd. J. W. Hebel. New York, 1930.

Devotions
Devotions upon Emergent Occasions, ed. John Sparrow. Cambridge, 1923.

Essays in Divinity
Essays in Divinity, ed. Evelyn M. Simpson. Oxford, 1952.

Ignatius his Conclave
Ignatius his Conclave, ed. Charles M. Coffin in *The Complete Poetry and Selected Prose of John Donne*. New York, 1952.

Paradoxes and Problems
Paradoxes and Problemes, ed. Geoffrey L. Keynes. London, 1923.

Pseudo-Martyr
Psevdo-Martyr. London, 1610.

Sermons
Sermons, ed. George R. Potter and Evelyn M. Simpson. 10 vols. Berkeley and Los Angeles, 1953–62.

Other abbreviations are:

Allen, "Renaissance Medicine"
D. C. Allen, "John Donne's Knowledge of Renaissance Medicine," *JEGP*, XLII (1943), 322–42.

Alsted
Ioannes Henricus Alstedius, *Scientiarum Omnium Encyclopaediae*. 2 vols. Lugduni, 1649.

Batman vppon Bartholome
Stephen Batman, *Batman vppon Bartholome*. London, 1582.

Cowell, *The Interpreter* — John Cowell, *The Interpreter, Wherein is Set Foorth such Words as are Mentioned in the Law Writers or Statutes of this Kingdome.* London, 1637.

Critici Sacri — *Critici Sacri, sive Doctissimorum Virorum in SS. Biblia Annotationes.* 7 vols. Francofurti, 1695–96.

Curtius, *European Literature* — Ernst R. Curtius, *European Literature and the Latin Middle Ages,* trans. Willard R. Trask. New York, 1953.

Gilbert, *De Magnete* — William Gilbert, *On the Loadstone and Magnetic Bodies,* trans. P. Fleury Mottelay. New York, 1893.

Gosse, *Life and Letters* — Edmund Gosse, *The Life and Letters of John Donne.* 2 vols. London, 1899.

Hakewill, *An Apologie* — George Hakewill, *An Apologie or Declaration of the Power and Providence of God.* London, 1630.

à Lapide, *Commentaria in Pentateuchum* — Cornelius à Lapide, *Commentaria in Pentateuchum Mosis.* Antuerpiae, 1681.

Paracelsus, *Opera* — Paracelsus, *Opera Omnia.* 3 vols. Genevae, 1669.

Paré, *Oeuvres* — Ambroise Paré, *Oeuvres.* Lyon, 1652.

Pererius — Benedictus Valentinus Pererius, *Commentariorum et Disputationum in Genesim.* Venetii, 1607.

PL — *Patrologia Latina,* ed. J. P. Migne. 221 vols. Parisorum, 1844–65.

Scaliger, *Exercitationes* — Julius Caesar Scaliger, *Exotericarum Exercitationum Liber XV de Subtilitate ad Hieronymum Cardanum.* Francofurti, 1607.

COMMENTARY

Title. In Renaissance poetic theory there were two main types of funeral elegy or *epitaphium* (the *oratio vel carmen* recited over the grave of the dead). One was the *epitaphium recens,* which lamented a recent death; the other, the *epitaphium anniversarium:*

> Epitaphia . . . anniuersaria esse possunt: quemadmodum Athenis, nam et Pericles dixit, extat apud Thucydidem. Plato quoque idem effecit. Item Aristidae tres scripti sunt. Est igitur Epitaphium, aut recens, aut anniuersarium. In recenti partes hae: Laudes, Iacturae demonstratio, Luctus, Consolatio, Exhortatio. In Anniuersario haec eadem omnia praeter luctum. Nemo enim iam annum bienniuḿue defunctum deflet. Multo verò minus si tantum temporis exactum sit, vt neque patres, neque liberi illius illoruḿue sit superstites. (Julius Caesar Scaliger, *Poetices* [n. p., 1581], pp. 425–26)

See also George Puttenham, *The Arte of English Poesie* in *Elizabethan Critical Essays,* ed. G. G. Smith (Oxford, 1904), II, 50; and *Much Ado About Nothing,* V, iii, 1–23, where Claudio "hangs an epitaph" on the tomb of Hero and vows at the end: "Now, unto thy bones good night! / Yearly will I do this rite." *The First Anniversary,* therefore, is not an anniversary in the strict sense of the word. Like Claudio's lament it is an epitaph which promises (lines 447–51) to become an anniversary through repeated performances. *The Second Anniversary,* on the other hand, is a true anniversary. It contains everything the epitaph does except grief.

Donne also uses the term in an ecclesiastical sense:

119

Those were of old called *Anniversary days,* whereon the martyrdoms
or death-days of Saints were celebrated yeerly in the Church; or the
days whereon at the yeers end, men were wont yeerly to pray for the
souls of their deceased friends according to the continued custom
of Roman Catholiques. (Thomas Blount, *Glossographia* [London,
1656], *s.v. Anniversary*)

Anatomies in the sixteenth and seventeenth centuries were
usually performed on the bodies of executed criminals. Cf.
Donne's "Vpon Mr. Thomas Coryats Crudities," 53–54; see
also Allen, "Renaissance Medicine," pp. 328–29.

TO THE PRAISE OF THE DEAD

Author. To the Praise of the Dead and the later *Harbinger to the
Progres* are usually attributed to Joseph Hall, although the only
actual evidence appears in the "Miscellanies" of Ben Jonson's
conversations with William Drummond of Hawthornden:
"Camden wrot that book remaines of Bretagne. / Joseph Hall
the Herbenger to Dones Anniversarie / the Epigrame of Martial
Vin Verpum he Vantes to expone" (*Works,* ed. C. H. Herford
and Percy Simpson [Oxford, 1925], I, 149). The statement is
somewhat ambiguous, but it apparently means that Hall wrote
the *Harbinger to the Progres.* It does not necessarily mean that
he also wrote the earlier *Praise of the Dead.* Yet there is no good
reason to believe that he did not, and there is no other likely
candidate. Other evidence in favor of Hall is somewhat more
tenuous. From 1601 to 1608 he had been rector of the church
on the Drury estate at Hawsted and consequently knew Elizabeth Drury's parents with some intimacy. The acquaintance
would seem to have ended in 1608, however, when Hall re-
signed his position after arguing with Sir Robert Drury over
an additional ten pounds a year he thought due him. Florence
S. Teager's contention (*PQ,* XV [1936], 412–13) that Hall
wrote the *Harbinger* to revenge himself on his ex-patron by
subtly ridiculing the extravagance of the *Anniversaries* is not

very likely. It does not give much credit to Donne's intelligence. A final bit of evidence in favor of Hall was discovered by Geoffrey Keynes, who pointed out that Samuel Macham was probably chosen as the publisher of the *Anniversaries* because of his acquaintance with Hall. Both were born in the town of Ashby de la Zouch, and both had already had business dealings together publishing Hall's earlier books (*Bibliography of Dr John Donne* [Cambridge, 1958], p. 134).

5: state. Property, possessions; estate.

14–18. The image is of a painting, and the language is dual. *Relate* in line 14 means not only to say or narrate, but also to bring into relation to or present, as a painting presents itself to one's eye. *Nephew* in line 15 is used in its Latin sense of *nepos*, a vague, remote descendant, but it is also used in its present sense, for Donne's poem is metaphorically a portrait which will be handed down in the family even to its last member. Similarly Donne's *cunning Pencill* is contrasted with the *vulgar pens* of line 20.

25–26. Cf. Ovid, *Amores*, I, xv, 39–40:

> Pascitur in vivis livor: post fata quiescit,
> Cum suus ex merito quemque tuetur honor.

27–30. The idea was apparently begun by Diodorus Siculus (I, 51). By the Renaissance it had become commonplace:

> Aegyptios legimus, praesigni magnificentia construere sepulchra con-sueuisse: quanquam in domorum aedificatione incuriosi admodum forent. Siquidem sepulchra defunctorum domos sempiternas, quonam apud inferos infinitum sit tempus, vocant. At domos ipsas, velut diuersoria opinantur, argumento vitae breuioris, ac momento tran-seuntis. (Ludovicus Caelius Rhodiginus, *Lectionum Antiquarum Libri Triginta* [Coloniae Allobrogum, 1620], p. 930)

See also Alexandrus ab Alexandro, *Genalium Dierum Libri Sex* (Parisiis, 1565), fol. 305a; Paré, *Oeuvres*, p. 775. The clay houses, however, are an addition. It was widely known that Egyptians lived in stone or wattle huts (Alexander ab Alexandro, fols. 305a–305b). The clay was probably added to make the image more applicable to the human body.

31–32. You gave us what we give you, so you may thank yourself for being thanked.

38: Amid the Quire of Saints and Seraphim. Not that all the saints are seated among the Seraphim, the highest of the nine angelic orders, but only those saints who, like her, have grace enough to deserve such an honor. Cf. Aquinas, *Summa*, I, Q. 108, a. 8, "Utrum homines assumantur ad ordines Angelorum." Arguing against Bonaventure and others who denied man's entry into the angelic hierarchies, Aquinas cites Matthew 24:30, that the saints "erunt sicut Angeli Dei in caelo," and concludes that "per donum gratiae homines mereri possunt tantam gloriam, ut Angelis aequentur secundum singulos Angelorum gradus; quod est homines ad ordines Angelorum assumi."

39. Whereas she and the Seraphim sing God's praises directly, the Angels, the lowest of the orders, praise God through their praise of her. The implication, of course, is that the Angel's tongue is also Donne's.

40: The subiects differ, tho the skill agree. Since she praises God and the Angels praise her, the subjects of the songs differ, yet the skill employed in each is the same (*agree*) so that they harmonize (*agree*).

44: burden. A pun meaning both a tiresome load and a refrain or chorus.

48: thy ditty, and thy note. The words of the song make up the ditty and the music or tune, the note. The *OED* cites Shake-

speare, *As You Like It*, V, iii, 36: "There was no great matter
in the dittie, yet ye note was very vntunable."

THE FIRST ANNIVERSARY

1: rich soule. I. A. Richards suggests two senses: "possessing
much (a rich man); giving much (a rich mine)" ("The Inter-
actions of Words" in *The Language of Poetry*, ed. Allan Tate
[Princeton, N.J., 1942], p. 81). Donne, however, supplies the
best gloss:

> Riches is the Metaphor, in which, the Holy Ghost hath delighted to
> expresse God and Heaven to us; *Despise not the riches of his good-*
> *nesse*, sayes the Apostle; And againe, *O the depth of the riches of his*
> *wisdome*; And so, after, *The unsearchable riches of Christ*; And for
> the consummation of all, *The riches of his Glory.* Gods goodnesse
> towards us in generall, our Religion in the way, his Grace here, his
> Glory hereafter, are all represented to us in Riches. (*Sermons*, VI,
> 303–04)

1: her Heauen. In the sense of being entirely hers, as it is
God's and at the same time only a degree of heaven, her particular
heaven, the one she had the capacity to fill. Cf. John 14:2: "In
my Father's house are many mansions: if it were not so, I would
have told you. I go to prepare a place for you" and Donne's
sermon on the text, VII, 118–40. See also *Sermons*, II, 253; VI,
335.

2: celebrate. Cf. "this is truly to glorifie God in his Saints, to
sanctifie our selves in their examples; To celebrate them, is to
imitate them" (*Sermons*, X, 190). According to the *OED* the
word *celebrate* was first used in the sense of praise, extoll, or
publish the fame of, around 1611. Earlier it had meant observe
with solemn rites or solemnize, as in the celebration of the
mass. Donne implies that all those who know they have a soul
glorify this "rich soule" by ritually reperforming it. The next

four lines expand the implication, and later, in lines 67–78, we learn that although she was the form of the old world, she is the matter and stuff of the new, which we inform.

3–6. To see, judge, and follow correspond to the three traditional faculties of the rational soul—memory, understanding, and will:

> As God, one *God* created us, so wee have a soul, *one soul*, that represents, and is some image of that one God; As the three Persons of the *Trinity* created us, so we have, in our one soul, a *threefold impression* of that image, and, as Saint *Bernard* calls it, *A trinity from the Trinity*, in those *three faculties* of the soul, the *Vnderstanding*, the *Will*, and the *Memory*. (*Sermons*, II, 72–73)

See also *Sermons*, III, 154; V, 149; Bernard, *PL* 184, 546–47; Peter Lombard, *PL* 192, 737. Although these constitute the image of God in man, the likeness is only potential until through grace the soul realizes itself and directs all its faculties toward God.

6: *In-mate*. A transient, an indigent lodger. The word had bad connotations. Cf. *Statutes of the Realm*, 35° Eliz. c. 6: "For the reformynge of the great Mischiefs and Inconveniences that daylie growe and increase by reason of the pesteringe of Houses with div'se Famylies, harboringe of Inmates, and convertinge of great Houses into sev'all Tĕnt̨ or Dwellings." See also E. M. Leonard, *The Early History of English Poor Relief* (Cambridge, 1900), pp. 73, 169–70; *Sermons*, VI, 350; II, 215.

7: *progresse*. Royal journey from one part of the kingdom to another.

8: *standing house*. The royal palace or permanent residence, as opposed to the temporary ones on progress. Cf. *Sermons*, VII, 137; VIII, 84.

9: attend. Wait for, look forward to, expect.

10: a part both of the Quire, and Song. Both a singer and the song sung, the praiser and the praised, just as later (lines 431–434) she is a partaker of the joys of heaven and a part.

11: This world, in that great earth-quake languished. The earthquake functions in terms of the microcosm-macrocosm analogy that informs the poem, but it is also an obscure remembrance of the death of Christ: "And behold, the veil of the temple was rent in twain from the top to the bottom; and the earth did quake, and the rocks rent" (Matthew 27:51). That is not to say, of course, that she is literally Christ. The allusion functions only as an overtone, and the same is true of similar allusions in the lines to come. Though they gradually become less subliminal and finally break the surface of the poetry, they remain symbolic, not allegorical: they make analogies, but not equations.

11: Languished. Original sin was traditionally described as languor; cf. Augustine, *De Civitate Dei*, XV, vi; *Biathanatos*, p. 38, which cites Aquinas' use of the term; and lines 99–102 below. Bernard uses it somewhat similarly: for him, *languor animi* (at times called *mentis hebetudo, inertia spiritus*) defined the state of the soul in the absence of the beloved (Etienne Gilson, *The Mystical Theology of Saint Bernard*, trans. A. H. C. Downes [London, 1940], pp. 104, 239).

12: in a common Bath of teares it bled. An extremely difficult image, obscure because of compression. The underlying idea is that eyes are to the body of the world as so many pores. The tears, therefore, bleed like bloody sweat, bathing the body in a common bath. It is not without reference to Christ's bath of blood in Gethsemane, when, according to Donne, *"non contentus lachrimis oculorum, totius corporis sanguineis lachrimis lachrimavit,* when besides his tears of water, he opened as many eyes as he had pores in his body, and wept out bloud at every one of those eyes" (*Sermons*, II, 161). The marginal note attributes the image to Ambrose, but according to Cornelius à Lapide, *Commentaria in Omnes Divi Pauli Epistolas* (Antuerpiae, 1692), p. 869, it is also to be found in Bernard. One of the standard glosses in the Renaissance was Theodore Beza's, which I believe works obscurely behind these lines. Beza argued that in assuming the nature of man Christ also assumed all the fears and weaknesses of man (*abiectas & infirmas hominis affectiones*), for in order to redeem him it was necessary to experience everything man was capable of experiencing, including the feeling of being deserted by God and cast out into darkness. In support of his argument Beza referred to two episodes in which Christ acted solely as man, not God. One was on the cross, when he felt himself deserted and cried out, "My God, my God, why hast thou forsaken me?" The other was in the garden of Gethsemane, when the burden of the sins of the world was so great that he was covered with a bloody sweat: "Peccata non unius hominis aliqua, sed omnium electorum omnia homo vnus ipse fragilis, caducus, imbecillis sustinet. Et miramur eum expauescere, consternari, turbari, lachrymari, clamere, repugnantia quodammodo petere, sanguinem sudore, se derelictum vociferari?" (*Novum D. N. Iesu Christi Testamentum* [n. p., 1557], fol. 289a). Donne seems to have telescoped both episodes in this image: like Christ on the cross the world in its agony feels itself deserted by God and at the same time the realization of its own guilt causes it to weep a sweat of blood.

13: vitall spirits.   The vital spirits were regarded as subtle substances of the blood which functioned as the bond between body and soul. Formed in the heart and disseminated by the arteries, they retained the body's innate heat. The bloody sweat of the previous image would naturally tend to exhaust them, whereby life would ebb and ultimately cease "as in a *syncope* or swouning" (Burton, *Anatomy of Melancholy*, I, i, 2, 2). See also John Swan, *Speculum Mundi* (Cambridge, 1643), p. 490; *Sermons*, II, 261–62; IV, 128; Allen, "Renaissance Medicine," p. 332.

14–20. The doubt and the subsequent flashes of fever are images of paradox used with considerable ambivalence to suggest the central paradox of Christianity, the *felix culpa*. For an excellent history of the idea, see A. O. Lovejoy, "Milton and the Paradox of the Fortunate Fall," *ELH*, IV (1937), 161–79.

21–24. Cf. "in Cramps which are contortions of the Sinewes, or in Tetars, which are rigors and stiffenesses in the Muscles, wee may procure to our selfe a feaver to thaw them, or we may procure them in a burning feaver, to condense and attemper our bloud againe" (*Biathanatos*, p. 171). According to the marginal note, the source of the information was Hippocrates' *Aphorisms*, II, 38 (IV, 57 in modern editions), but it was apparently a commonplace: cf. *Batman vppon Bartholome* fol. 91b. The idea is that the rigorous convulsions of grief immediately after the loss gave way to another disease of half-hope, half-despair, which cured the first and in time even spent itself. But it produced the secondary disease of forgetfulness, which is killing the patient.

24: Letargee. Cf.

> Consider the evil of this security you are in, of this disposition of heart, when you cry, peace, peace, to your selves in the midst of Gods displeasure. It is an evil disease, a spiritual Lethargy. That disease we know in the body, it takes a man with sleep, and so he dieth. . . . It is more dangerous, because it is a senseless disease, a disease that takes the senses from the soul: and diseases (we know) that take away the senses, are dangerous: for it is not onely a sign that nature is overcome by the disease, but besides, it draweth men from seeking for cure. Thus it is with the spiritual Lethargy; it shews not only that sin hath prevailed in the heart . . . , but it hindereth you from seeking the means to escape out of it. (ΘΡΗΝΟΙΚΟΣ: *The House of Mourning* [London, 1672], p. 155)

See also *Sermons,* II, 239; III, 56, 365; V, 233; IX, 381.

25–42. The concern with the name in the lines that follow is a symbolic action that names her—not explicitly, but obliquely. For it is impossible for those in a state of spiritual lethargy to remember their name, their own identity. She is the opposite of the world's disease. She is the *Word:* the soul's ability to speak and call upon God. Cf.

> *Inter caeteras Dei appellationes, Sermonem veneramur,* Amongst Gods other Names, we honour that, that he is *the Word;* That implies a Communication, Gods goodnesse in speaking to us, and an obligation upon us, to speake to him. . . . Upon men that are dumb, that is, speechlesse in avowing him, God heaps other mischievous impediments too; Deafnesse, They shall not heare him in his word, and Blindnesse, They shall not see him in his works. (*Sermons,* VIII, 119)

She is the Word made flesh in us:

> There is first [in conversation with God] an open profession of the tongue required; And therefore the Holy Ghost descended in fiery tongues, *Et lingua propria Spiritui Sancto,* sayes S. *Gregory,* The tongue is the fittest Instrument for the Holy Ghost to worke upon, and to worke by, *Qui magnam habet cognationem cum Verbo,* sayes he, The Son of God is the Word, and the Holy Ghost proceeds from him, And because that faith that unites us to God, is expressed in the tongue, howsoever the heart be the center in which the Holy Ghost rests, the tongue is the Spheare, in which he moves . . . ; Christ is not borne in us, we are not regenerate in him, if we delight not to speake of his wondrous mercyes, and infinite goodnesse to the sons of men; as soone as he is borne in us, his Spirit speakes in us, and by us; in which, our first profession is *Iesum esse,* That Jesus is, That there is a Jesus. (*Sermons,* VI, 122)

See also *Sermons,* II, 239; V, 386; VI, 71, 281, 347. In more traditional terms, not under pressure of the immediate metaphor of speechlessness, she is *sapientia creata.* Cf. "Christ, who is *Sapientia Dei,* the wisdome of God, is *Verbum, Sermo Dei,* the

word of God, he is the wisdome, and the uttering of the wisdome of God" (Sermons, II, 228; see also V, 113). For the
classic statement of the relationship between the word and
wisdom see Aquinas, Commentum in Quatuor Libros Sententiarum, I, d. 34, q. 2:

> Unde si consideretur sapientia apud nos secundum quod consistit in
> cognitione conclusionis quae mente accipitur, sic est idem quod
> verbum mentis; si autem consideretur sapientia secundum quod con-
> sistit in lumine intellectus agentis et cognitione primarum princi-
> piorum, sic praecedit verbum, quod est conceptio conclusionis. . . .
> Ita etiam est in divinis: quia ipsa sapientia genita est idem quod
> verbum.

The wisdom Donne has in mind is of the second type. It precedes
the Word, though the Word is its expression. See also Rabanus
Maurus, PL 111, 709–10; Biblia Latina, cum postillis Nicolai
de Lyra et additionibus Pauli Burgensis (Nuremberg, 1497), II,
246b; Cornelius à Lapide, Commentaria in Salomonis Proverbia
(Antuerpiae, 1681), p. 15; Sebastian Munster, Isidorus Clarius,
Rodolphus Baynus, cited in Critici Sacri, III, 87, 89, 94.

At the same time, of course, Donne also implies the name
Adonai, the ineffable name of God in the Tetragrammaton. See
the Introduction under the discussion of the Shekinah.

25: Her death did wound, and tame thee than. Original sin
was traditionally described as a wound. Cyprian probably originated the metaphor (PL, 4, 625–26), but Aquinas codified it:

> per justitiam originalem perfecte ratio continebat inferiores animae
> vires; et ipsa ratio a Deo perficiebatur ei subjecta. Haec autem ori-
> ginalis justitia subtracta est per peccatum primi parentis. . . .
> Et ideo omnes vires animae remanent quodammodo distitutae proprio
> ordine, quo naturaliter ordinantur ad virtutem; et ipsa distitutio
> vulneratio naturae dicitur. (Summa, I–II, Q. 85, a. 3)

See also Ambrose, *PL* 14, 1058; Anselm, *PL* 158, 395; Quarles, *Emblems*, II, 13; Milton, *Paradise Lost*, IX, 781–784; *Dictionnaire de Théologie Catholique*, *s.v. Péché Originel*. Cf.

> in that wound, as wee were all shot in *Adam*, we bled out *Impassibilitatem*, and we sucked in *Impossibilitatem;* There we lost our *Immortality*, our *Impassibility*, our assurance of Paradise, and then we lost *Possibilitatem boni*, says S. *Augustine:* all possibility of recovering any of this by our selves. (*Sermons*, II, 55)

32: and her thou hast o'repast.   Since she was your identity, you have outlived your own death. Cf. "Thou pursueth the works of the flesh, and hast none . . . ; Dissolution and putrefaction is gone over thee alive; Thou has over liv'd thine own death, and art become thine own ghost, and thine own hell" (*Sermons*, II, 83).

33–36.   The image proceeds naturally from the previous references to the loss of grace. We are not only given our own names in baptism, we are also regenerated into Christ's name; "Neither is there salvation in any other: for there is none other name under heaven given among men, whereby we must be saved" (Acts 4:12; see also *Sermons*, V, 164–65; VI, 137).

37–38.   John 1:1,3: "In the beginning was the Word, and the Word was with God, and the Word was God. . . . All things were made by him; and without him was not any thing made that was made." This was also traditionally associated with Wisdom:

> When God therefore prepared the heavens, there he was, and there was his Eternall Wisdome, there, in the working and preparing of them. When having drawn that circumference, he set his compasse upon the face of the depth, then also there in the compassing of it, was the Eternall Wisdome, the rule and compasse of his working. . . . Surely he it is who is the worker in them all. He it is who invented and framed the great Cymball of the world, which is but so many circumferences and spheares set one within the other, and

whereby the musicke of Gods praise, is most sweetly and fully sounded out. (Michael Jermin, *Paraphrasticall Meditations . . . upon the Whole Booke of the Proverbs of Solomon* [London, 1638], p. 169)

39–42. After death, time ceases to exist and measures of it end. Therefore we can speak of her death of only a few months ago as the same as almost six thousand years ago, which is how long what she represents has been away. An overt reference to the fact that the subject of these poems (in the sense of what they are about) is not Elizabeth Drury.

40: determined. Come to an end, ceased, expired.

48: A strong example gone equall to law. The force of her example was as strong as a law. The idea is that laws are binding, whereas examples are not, and perhaps also that laws are universals and therefore more important than particulars. Cf. "All wayes of teaching, are Rule and Example: And though ordinarily the Rule be first placed, yet the Rule it selfe is made of Examples" (*Sermons*, IX, 274).

51: some blasphemy. A degree of blasphemy, used figuratively in the sense of an impious speech against something held sacred.

57: Thy'ntrinsique Balme, and thy preseruatiue. Cf.

Physitians say, That man hath in his Constitution, in his Complexion, a naturall vertue, which they call *Balsamum suum*, his owne Balsamum, by which, any wound which a man could receive in his body, would cure it selfe. . . . Something that hath some proportion and analogy to this Balsamum of the body, there is in the soule of man too: The soule hath *Nardum suam*, her Spikenard . . . , a naturall disposition to Morall goodnesse, as the body hath to health. (*Sermons*, V, 347–48)

In another sermon Donne explains that "We are so far from that naturall Balsamum, as that we have a naturall poyson in us, Originall sin" (VI, 116). Donne got the material for the metaphor from the new physic of Paracelsus and his disciples: *"Balsamum, est substantia corporum, à putredine conservans. . . . Est internus, & externus.* Internus in humano corpore, temperatissima quaedam est substantia non amara, non dulcis, non acerba, neque Sal minerale, sed sal liquoris, quod à putrefactione validissimè praeservat humana corpora" (William Johnson, *Lexicon Chymicum* [Londini, 1660], p. 42). See also Paracelsus, *Opera*, III, 30 and the glossary of terms at the end of the volume.

70–76. The remembrance is weak and fading, like the light after sunset, but nevertheless powerful enough to beget something from nothingness, like Hamlet's sun breeding maggots in a dead dog, "being a god kissing carrion" (II, ii, 181–82). For the widespread belief in the sun's generative powers, see Aristotle, *Physics*, 194b 14; Ovid, *Meta.*, I, 422–43; Spenser *FQ*, III, vi, 5–8, 11 and the *Variorum* notes in volume I, 184–87.

76: a new world. It is clear from lines 81–82 that this new world is the traditional Paradise within. Cf.

> that man, who hath taken hold of God, by those handles, by which God hath delivered, and manifested himselfe in the notions of Father, Sonne and holy Ghost; he is no field, but a garden, a Garden of Gods planting, a Paradise in which grow all things good to eate, and good to see, (spirituall refection, and spirituall recreation too) and all things good to cure. (*Sermons*, XI, 51–52)

See also Augustine, *De Civitate Dei*, XIII, xxi; Iacobus Merlo Horstius, *Paradisus Animae Christianae* (Coloniae Agrippinae, 1644); Milton, *Paradise Lost*, XII, 585–87.

81–84. An allusion to the ancient exegetical problem of whether the roses in Eden had thorns and the snakes venom. Most commentators in the Renaissance believed that they did, but that they were harmless until after the fall (Pererius, pp. 48, 118; à Lapide, *Commentaria in Pentateuchum*, p. 53; Arnold Williams, *The Common Expositor: An Account of the Commen-*

taries on Genesis, 1527–1633 [Chapel Hill, N.C., 1948], pp. 108–09). Some, however, agreed with Donne that they were contrary to the perfection of the first creation (J. H. Hottinger, ΚΤΙΣΙΣ ΕΞΑΗΜΕΡΟΣ: *Id est; Historiae Creationis Examen* [Heidelbergae, 1659], p. 232).

81: assum'd. Chosen, elected, with the additional idea of being taken up or elevated.

91–171. Donne's use of the topic of the decay of the world in this and the following sections is by and large traditional. For a history of the idea in Greek and Roman literature, see Arthur O. Lovejoy, *et al., A Documentary History of Primitivism and Related Ideas* (Baltimore, 1935). For its continuation in the Renaissance, see George Hakewill, *An Apologie or Declaration of the Power and Providence of God* (London, 1630); Godfrey Goodman, *The Fall of Man* (London, 1616); Victor Harris, *All Coherence Gone* (Chicago, 1949); R. F. Jones, *Ancients and Moderns* (St. Louis, 1936); George Williamson, "Mutability, Decay, and Seventeenth-Century Melancholy," *ELH*, II (1935), 121–50; D. C. Allen, "The Degeneration of Man and Renaissance Pessimism," *SP*, XXXV (1938), 202–27. The history of the idea in the Middle Ages has not yet been written, but a few of the more important primary sources are: Cyprian, *PL* 4, 561–84, 623; Lactantius, *PL* 6, 779–93; Augustine, *PL* 42, 447–48; Gregory, *PL* 76, 1079–80; Fredegarius, *MGH, SRM*, II, 123; Hugh of St. Victor, *PL* 176, 713, 720; Richard of St. Victor, *PL* 196, 201–12; Innocent III, *PL* 217, 706, 715; Aquinas, *Commentum in Quatuor Libros Sententiorum*, I, d. xi, q. 1; Chaucer, *The Clerk's Tale*, 1135–40.

91–95. Psalm 38:1–3: "O Lord, rebuke me not in thy wrath: neither chasten me in thy hot displeasure. For thine arrows stick fast in me, and thy hand presseth me sore. There is no soundness in my flesh because of thine anger; neither is there any rest in my bones because of my sin." Cf. Donne's sermon on the text, particularly:

God created man in health, but health continued but a *few hours,* and sicknesse hath had the Dominion 6000 years. . . . And no sicknesse can be worse, then that which is intended here, for it is all over, *Non sanitas, no soundnesse,* no health in any part. This consideration arises . . . [partly] from the Physicians Rule, that the best state of Mans body is but a *Neutrality,* neither well nor ill, but *Nulla sanitas,* a state of true and exquisit health, say they, no man hath. . . . *Non sanitas,* there is *never* any soundness in us; for, *semper deficimus;* we are *Borne* in a *Consumption,* and as *little* as we are then, we grow less from that time. *Vita cursus ad mortem;* Before we can craule, we runne to meet death. (II, 79–80)

The physician's rule on neutrality was a scientific commonplace; see Allen, "Renaissance Medicine," p. 327.

95–98. Cf.

What miserable revolutions and changes, what downfals, what break-necks, and precipitations may we justly think our selves ordained to, if we consider, that in our comming into this world out of our mothers womb, we doe not make account that a childe comes right, except it come with the head forward, and thereby prefigure that headlong falling into calamities which it must suffer after? (*Sermons,* VI, 333)

See also *Sermons,* V, 171.

95: ruinous. Falling into ruin (a rare seventeenth-century usage), linking it with the precipitation of lines 97–98. Cf. Milton's "Hell saw / Heav'n ruining from Heav'n" (*Paradise Lost,* VI, 867–68) or Spenser's "huge cave . . . / From whose rough vaut the ragged breaches hong . . . / That heavy ruine they did seeme to threatt" (*FQ,* II, vii, 28).

98: precipitation. A pun on the etymology: *praeceps* > *prae* + *caput, headfirst.*

102: reliefe. *In adjutorium,* as a helpmeet, with slight sexual overtones.

104: accessory, and principall. Women are only accessory (*adjutores,* helpers) in good, but in evil they are the principals. Cf.

> *Accessory (Accessorius vel Accessorium)* is used in our common law, otherwise then among the Civilians. Forwhereas with them it is generally taken for any thing depending upon another: here though it be so likewise, yet most commonly and notoriously it signifieth a man that is guilty of a fellonious offence, not principally, but by participation: as by commandment, advice or concealement. (Cowell, *The Interpreter, s.v. Accessory*)

106: One woman at one blow, then kill'd vs all. This is traditionally applied to Adam. Cf. Romans 5:12: "Wherefore, as by one man sin entered into the world, and death by sin; and so death passed upon all men; for that all have sinned." The usual exposition is Augustine's: "Quia secundum propaginem carnis in illo eramus omnes, antequam nati essemus, tanquam in parente, tanquam in radice ibi eramus: sic venenata est ista arbor, ubi eramus" (*PL* 38, 344). It was echoed by Donne in his sermons: "man was sowr'd in the lumpe, poysoned in the fountaine, withered in the roote, in the loins of *Adam*" (*Sermons,* IV, 148).

107: kill. The usual seventeenth-century pun on *die.*

109: profusely. A pun of sorts: *profundere = pour out.* Cf. "we profuse and poure out even our own soule" (*Sermons,* V, 297).

110: We kill our selues, to propagate our kinde. It was a popular and scientific commonplace that coitus shortens life: "calor naturalis in humiditate existit naturali, et ab ea nutritur; et cum humiditas illa dissoluitur, calor minuitur et debilitatur . . . ; coitus plurimus et flebotomia plurima . . . faciunt . . . viam dissolutionis naturalis humiditatis" (Roger Bacon, *De Retarda-*

tione Accidentium Senectutis, ed. A. G. Little and E. Withington [Oxonii, 1928], pp. 86, 46). For similar statements from the Renaissance, see Allen, "Renaissance Medicine," pp. 335–36.

113–114. "*Ioynt tenants (simul tenentes)* . . . bee those that come to and hold Lands or Tenements by one title *pro indiviso,* or without partition . . . ; they that have equall right in lands and tenements, and all by vertue of one title" (Cowell, *The Interpreter, s.v. Ioynt tenants* and *Tenementis legatis*). Since both the sun and man had the right to the property by the same title, neither could become sole owner except by the death of the other. Consequently the strife to see who could live longest.

115: Stag, and Rauen, and the long-liu'd tree. In a fragment of Hesiod's preserved in paraphrase by Pliny (*Nat. Hist.,* VII, 48) and Ausonius (*Idyllium* XVIII, 1–6) deer are said to have lived four times longer than ravens and ravens four times longer than men. The long-lived tree was probably added by Ausonius: "Quam vos perpetuo decies praevertitis aevo, / Nymphae Hamadryades, quarum longissima vita est" (7–8). In the Renaissance, however, there was confusion about the tree. Jean Bodin thought it was the palm (*Method for the Easy Comprehension of History,* trans. Beatrice Reynolds [New York, 1945], p. 109); Hakewill and Donne, the oak (*An Apologie,* p. 30; *Sermons,* IX, 149).

117–120. Cf. Josephus, *Antiquities,* I, iv, 9:

> God afforded them [the first men] a longer time of life on account of . . . the good use they made of it in astronomical and geometrical discoveries, which would not have afforded the time for foretelling unless they had lived six hundred years; for the great year is completed in that interval.

By Donne's time it was a commonplace; see Hakewill, *An Apologie,* p. 40.

120: obseruation. Probably also in the specific sense of the longitude or latitude of a star obtained by taking its altitude with an astronomical instrument.

122: Man's grouth confess'd, and recompenc'd the meat. **Meat** is used in the archaic sense of food in general. It was commonly believed that the food of the Patriarchs was much better than that of later years, partly because of God's curse on the land in Genesis 3:17–18, and partly because of the salt in the soil after the Deluge. See Arnold Williams, *The Common Expositor* (Chapel Hill, N.C., 1948), p. 147 and Hakewill, *An Apologie,* pp. 34–35. Man's growth, therefore, *confessed* the meat by showing how good it was, and it *recompenced* it by adding as many pounds as were eaten.

125–126. Donne's version of the *topos homo erectus.* Cf. Cicero, *De Legibus,* I, ix, 26: "Nam quum ceteras animantes abiecisset ad pastum, solum hominem erexit ad caelique, quasi cognationis domicilique pristini, conspectum excitavit"; see also Ovid, *Meta.,* I, 84–86; Cyprian, *PL* 4, 575–76; and Chaucer, *Troilus,* V, 1837–41. The extra fillip, characteristic of Donne, is apparently his own. Cf.

> Wee attribute but one privilege and advantage to Mans body, above other moving creatures, that he is not as others, groveling, but of an erect, of an upright form, naturally built, and disposed to the contemplation of Heaven. Indeed it is a thankfull forme, and recompences that *soule,* which gives it, with carrying that soule so many foot higher, towards *heaven.* (*Devotions,* p. 10)

130: new made. The reading *true made* is obviously tautological: if a clock were true, there would be no sense in testing it. Grierson, however, in a reply to John Sparrow's publication of the 1612 errata, defended it somewhat (*TLS,* 20 July 1946). He believed that his collation was correct and that the reading of the errata was a correction of the original. He accepted it as such but protested that "one would have hesitated to accept it if merely a conjecture, for a new made clock might show its defects early." But that is precisely the point. The lines must be read against lines 117–20 to find their full meaning. The idea is that everything has shrunk; instead of studying the awesome wheeling of the new made firmament for two or three hundred years, men now study the movements of new made clocks and die almost before the end of a day.

134: In a torne house, or field, to haue three liues. As Grosart suggests *torne* is a pun of sorts on rented. The man is a tenant with a lease for ninety-nine years, or, as it is still called in England, three lives. But it is also used in the figurative sense of ragged. Cf. "A Hymne to Christ," line 1: "In what torne ship soever I embarke."

135–144. The traditional belief in giants was thought to have been corroborated in the Renaissance by actual archeological evidence. Monstrous bones of the ancients were discovered in almost all the scientific excavations. At Rome, for example, the "body" of Pallas, Evander's son, was discovered in the year 1500 and was found to be as high as the city walls (Hieronymous Magius, *Miscellaneorum, seu Variarum Lectionum* in *Lampas, sive Fax Artium Liberalium,* ed. Ianus Gruterus [Francofurti, 1605], II, 1271–72). For an excellent survey, see D. C. Allen, "Donne among the Giants," *MLN,* LXI (1946), 257–60.

141–143. Pygmies were thought to be imaginary creatures. Cf. "Naturall men will write of lands of Pygmies . . . ; But yet advisedly they do not beleeve, (at least confidently they do not know) that there are . . . such Pygmies . . . in the world" (*Sermons,* IX, 100–101). Gellius and Rhodogin thought they were a kind of ape; Strabo, Cassanion, and Cardan believed that they were simply lying fables (Hakewill, *An Apologie,* p. 9).

143–146. Cf. Donne's "Lecture upon the Shadow."

145: Onely death addes t'our length. A difficult phrase, but I think it is to be understood in terms of the image itself: in death our height, that is, our vertical position, turns into length, since we are laid out horizontally, just as the sun in its zenith casts only pools of shadows, which lengthen out in the afternoon as the sun itself declines toward death.

148-149: or had we chang'd to gold / Their siluer. Not only a reference to alchemy, but also to the ages of the world. The Patriarchs lived in the silver, Adam and Eve in the golden age.

149: dispos'd into lesse glas. Either distillation or sublimation.

151: w'are not retir'd, but dampt. In context *retir'd* apparently means something like reduced from quantity to quality, but the OED has no mention of such a usage. The closest thing offered is contracted or shrunk, and that is questioned since there is only one puzzling citation: Ben Jonson, *Volpone*, II: "Crampes, Convulsions, Paralysies, Epilepsies, Tremor-cordia, retired-Nerues." *Dampt* means stifled, extinguished, dulled, or deadened.

159-160. Syphilis, which overran Europe in the fifteenth century, was the most startling of these new diseases. *New phisicke* refers to the new breed of doctors led by Paracelsus, who boasts in *Ignatius his Conclave* (p. 325) that he "broght all *Methodicall Phisitians,* and the art it selfe into so much contempt, that that kind of phisick is almost lost." In the verse Donne apparently thinks he is using Paracelsus' own words against him. Cf. *Biathanatos,* p. 215:

as *Paracelsus* says, of that foule contagious disease [syphilis] which than had invaded mankind in a few places, and since overflowen in all, that for punishment of generall licentiousnes, God first inflicted that disease, and when the disease would not reduce us, he sent a second worse affliction, which was ignorant, and torturing Physitians.

Although I spent a considerable amount of time, I was unable to find this statement in Paracelsus' works. He believed that syphilis was a punishment from God: "esse autem morbos ac vlcera peccatorum poenas, Morbus Gallicus argumento est"; and he also thought that other doctors were killers: "huiusmodi Medicus non medicus, sed Carnifex dici et proclamari debet. . . . Huic & suis remediis, vel nouos induxêre morbos, vel illos ipsos longe graviores efficêre" (*Opera*, II, 65, 108, 49). But so far as I know he never said exactly what Donne quotes. Perhaps, however, Donne is not quoting from Paracelsus directly but from his own notes, which would account for his telescoping scattered statements.

161: this worlds Vice-Emperor.   In Genesis I:26, 28, God made man his viceroy when He gave him "dominion over the fish of the sea, and over the cattle, and over all the earth, and over every creeping thing that creepeth upon the earth."

171–174.   Grant whatever you want to man's other wants; give him help or at least some time to waste (both the time and himself). No matter what you grant will be useless because he lost his heart, and (as we learn from the end of this section, line 186) "The heart being perish'd, no part can be free." The metaphor of the heart is based on a medical commonplace:

> "coeur de l'homme, lequel côme il est le commencement de vie & de mouuement, aussi faut-il viure & mouuoir tous les autres membres; que s'il vient à estre blessé le mouuement qui estoit par tout les corps ne cesse pas seulement, mais aussi la vie: & en suite on peut voir Hypocrate, qui confirme tellement ceste doctrine. (Jacques Gaffarel, *Curiositez Inouyes* [n. p., 1637], pp. 137–38)

See also Pietro Andrea Mattioli, *Opera Omnia* (Basileae, 1674), p. 974. Cf. "the heart is that part that lives first and dyes last" (*Sermons*, I, 192; see also VII, 283 and I, 179–80, 204). Donne never tired of repeating the metaphor; throughout his life it remained one of his favorites:

man hath lost his *paratum cor meum;* he cannot say, *his heart is prepared;* that he hath lost in originall sin. . . . . He hath lost his *variis odoribus delectatum cor,* the delight which his heart heretofore had in the savour of the field, in those good actions, in which formerly he exercised himself, and now is falne from: But yet there may be *cor novum, a new heart,* a heart which is yet in Gods bosome, and shall be transplanted into his. (*Sermons,* VII, 113)

See also *Sermons,* I, 179, 181; IX, 314; V, 357–58; VII, 188, 283; VI, 129.

173: depart. Both give up, surrender and go away from. When she died, men necessarily parted with her, but the underlying implication is that men caused her loss by abandoning her.

175–176. Like most abstractions in Greek and Latin the names of virtues are in the feminine gender.

180: The poysonous tincture. By identifying it with original sin Donne violently perverted the alchemical use of tincture. Cf.

Tinctura, est arcanum specificum cum essentia & qualitatibus formalibus etiam colorem rei habens, ut in sui similem naturam tingere possit. Neque tam elaborandi gratia petitur, quam efficaciter ad sui naturam immutandi, quantum dispositio rei patitur. Itaque in medicina plurium ad valetudinis restaurationem, & sanitatem firmendam adhibetur, ita ut ob validam virtutem etiam renovandi potestatem habere dicatur, cum omnia membra; sanguinem spiritum & calorem reddat, usu sui vegetum & valentem. (William Johnson, *Lexicon Chymicum* [Londini, 1660], pp. 231–32)

187–190. Cf.

Now, as the end of all bodily eating, is Assimilation, that after all other concoctions, that meat may be made *Idem corpus,* the same body that I am; so the end of all spirituall eating, is Assimilation too, That after all Hearing, and all Receiving, I may be made *Idem spiritus cum Domino,* the same spirit, that my God is. (*Sermons,* VI, 223)

See also *Sermons,* VII, 280; II, 291.

187: feed (not banquet). Eat, not pick at. *Banquet* is used in its common seventeenth-century meaning of a dessert of nuts, fruit, and wine.

192: almost created lame. The creation of the Angels was generally accepted to have been God's first act, and since they fell almost immediately, they were corrupt before any other creatures were made. Augustine apparently began the tradition in his *De Genesi ad Litteram.* Genesis had failed to mention how or when the Angels were created, but Augustine included them under the creation of light: "primo die, quo lux facta est, conditionem spiritualis et intellectualis creaturae lucis appellatione intimari [potet]—in qua natura intelleguntur omnes sancti angeli atque uirtutes" (II, 8). Cf.

> We know that light is Gods eldest childe, his first borne of all Creatures; and it is ordinarily received, that the Angels are twins with the light, made then when light was made. And then the first act, that these Angels that fell, did, was an act of Pride. . . . So early, so primary a sin is Pride, as that it was the first act of the first of Creatures. (*Sermons,* II, 294)

See also *Sermons,* X, 180. The instantaneousness of the Angels' fall entered the tradition by way of Augustine's discussion of their morning and evening knowledge as adopted and elaborated by Aquinas; see the notes to *The Second Anniversary,* line 446.

197: And turn'd her braines. The Angels were regarded as pure intellect, as Donne puts it, the brains of the world, and by their fall they became addled.

198: wronging. Bennett for some reason amends this to *wringing.*

201–202. A complex recapitulation of lines 191–200 referring to the immediate fall of the Angels and offering Donne's own gloss for the Hebrew idiom (Genesis I:5) "And the evening and the morning were the first day." The obvious irrationality of this phrase, which ended each day of the creation week, had caused considerable difficulty for exegetes. Most of them simply supplied *catenae* of conflicting opinions (Pererius, pp. 30–31; Guilielmus Estius, *Annotationes Aureae* [Coloniae Agrippinae, 1622], pp. 2–3). Donne's explanation is witty and fantastic, but it is also curiously similar to a number of Medieval interpretations, which identified the first evening as the darkness of man's sin:

> Quare in primo die non posuit mane, vel in septimo die vesperam? Ideo mane non posuit, quia praevidit hominem peccantem in paradiso, et nox ignorantiae eum secuta fuit; et in septimo ideo non posuit vesperam, quia praesciebat eum ad veniam reversum fuisse per adventum Salvatoris. (Pseudo-Bede, *PL* 93, 221)

See also *PL* 112, 1467–68; *PL* 178, 295.

204: Like sonnes of women after fifty bee. As Grosart notes, "—*i.e.* none at all, fifty being held to be woman's limit in childbearing." But Donne also has in mind Esdras 5:51–55:

> Ask a woman who bears children, and she will tell you. For if you say to her, 'Why are those whom you have borne lately not like those whom you bore before but smaller in stature?' she herself will tell you, 'Those who were born in the vigor of youth are of one kind, and those who were born in old age, when the womb was failing, are of another.' So you too must consider that you are smaller in stature than those who were before you, and those who come after you will be smaller than you, for the creation is already growing old, as it

were, and past the strength of youth. (Edgar J. Goodspeed, trans. [Chicago, 1939])

205: And new Philosophy cals all in doubt. For an excellent gloss on the entire section, see Robert Burton's "Degression of Ayre" in *The Anatomy of Melancholy*, II, ii, 3. Other than Donne no one presents more clearly the impact of scientific rationalism on the Medieval world picture.

206: The Element of fire is quite put out. Cf.

> Against the popular opinion of the Spheare, or Element of Fire, some new Philosophers have made this an argument, that it is improbable, and impertinent, to admit an Element that produceth no Creatures; A matter more subtill then all the rest, and yet work upon nothing in it; A region more spacious then all the rest, and yet have nothing in it, to worke upon. All the other three Elements, Earth, and Water, and Ayre abound with inhabitants proper to each of them, onely the Fire produces nothing. (*Sermons*, VII, 184)

See also *Sermons*, IX, 230–31; Pererius, pp. 22–23. Burton (II, ii, 3) lists P. Nonius Saluciensis and Kepler in favor of the popular opinion, Cardan, Tycho, and John Pena, opposed.

209–212. Donne turns the optimism of the founders of modern astronomy to pessimism: the only reason they search so diligently for new worlds is that they know this one is finished. But the lines also involve the problem of the plurality of worlds. According to Burton (II, ii, 3), Kepler believed that there were *"Joviall and Saturnine inhabitants"*; Cardinal Cusanus, Walkarinus, Bruno, Pythagoras, Aristarchus, Samius, Heraclitus, Epicurus, Melissus, Democritus, Leucippus all "maintained in their ages, there be infinite earths or systems, *in infinito aethere*"; Thomas Campanella thought that the sun and moon were inhabited, "but with what kind of creatures, he cannot say." Perhaps they were like "those two green children, which Nubrigensis speaks of in his time, that fell from heaven." See also Milton, *Paradise Lost*, III, 561–571.

211–212. According to Epicurus, atoms were solid, impenetrable, indestructible objects which composed the matter of the universe. The only other element was void. But Donne is not actually concerned with atomic theory in these lines; he simply uses it to make the point that things fall apart, just as he is not theologically concerned when he implies by using the word *again* that chaos (Ovid's "Non bene junctarum discordia semina rerum," *Meta.*, I, 9) existed before creation. See also Vergil, *Ecl.*, VI, 31–33.

216–218. The phoenix was one of the favorite tropes of Renaissance biographers. Cf. Iacobus Philippus Tomasinus, *Petrarcha Redivuus* (Patavii, 1650), p. 1: "Nec sane mihi quicquam carius fuit, quàm post Historici Principis monumenta [Livy] *Petrarchae* Poetarum & Oratorum aeui sui Phoenicis gloriam propagare."

219–222. As Charles M. Coffin noted (*John Donne and the New Philosophy* [New York, 1938], pp. 84–87), these lines refer directly to William Gilbert's *De Magnete* (1600). According to Gilbert the world in its first form possessed a magnetic *anima mundi:*

> This form is unique and peculiar . . . ; it is the form of the prime and principal globes; and it is of the homogeneous and not altered parts thereof, the proper entity and existence which we may call the primary, radical, and astral form; not Aristotle's prime form, but that unique form which keeps and orders its own globe. (p. 105)

220: bow. Incline, turn, direct.

223–226. Moving from magnetism to its effect in the compass, Donne subverts one of the standard proofs of progress in the

Renaissance. Printing, the compass, and gunpowder were considered the only genuine contributions to knowledge made since the time of the ancients. Cf.

> Outre la restitution presqu'accomplie du sçavoir ancien, l'invention de plusieurs belles choses nouvelles . . . a esté reservée à cest aage. Entre lesquelles l'Imprimerie merite d'estre mise la premiere par son excellence. . . . La second louenge doit estre donne a l'invention de la boete marine, rose, & esquille d'acier, laquelle touchee ou frottee sur la pierre d'aymant, monstre tousjours la point respondant au lieu ou l'on imagine la pole arctique. . . . Par cest' adresse tout l'Ocean a esté navigué, isles innumerables trouvées, & descouverte grande partie de la terre ferme ver Occident & Midy, incogneuë aux anciens. . . . Je donnerais volontiers le troisieme lieu a la Bombarde ou Canonerie. (Loys Le Roy, *De la Vicissitude*, ed. Blanchard W. Bates [Princeton, 1944], pp. 29–31)

See also Hakewill, *An Apologie*, pp. 272–88; Jean Bodin, *Method for the Easy Comprehension of History*, trans. Beatrice Reynolds (New York, 1945), p. 301. The standard book on the subject was Guido Pancirolli's *Rerum Memorabilium*, edited by Henry Salmuth.

229: Steward. Cf. "There are two things required of every Steward. First, a Dispensation. Secondly, a right ordering of his Dispensation. . . . For a *Steward* ye know is appointed for laying out, he is made for others, not for himself, for the good of the Family in which he is set, not for his own benefit" (ΘΡΗΝΟΙΚΟΣ: *The House of Mourning* [London, 1672], p. 2). Cf. also *The Progresse of the Soule*, line 31: "Great Destiny the Commissary of God" and *A Funerall Elegie*, lines 95–96.

234: single money. Small change. Cf. "Hath he [God] changed his blessings unto me into single mony? Hath he made me rich by half pence and farthings?" (*Sermons*, III, 345; see also VI, 275 and *Devotions*, p. 67).

239–246. Donne has in mind specifically a hectic fever which has reached its third and last degree of intensity. Cf.

"Le *premier* degré donc, est quand la chaleur hectique consomme l'humidité des parties solides. Le *second,* quand il deuore la substance charneuse d'icelles. Le *troisiesme* & dernier qui est incurable, quand il s'attache aux parties solides, & les destruit & consomme. Tout ainsi que la flamme d'vue lampe consomme premierement l'huyle, en apres la propre humidité du lumignon, & en fin le corps du lumignon mesme; ce qu'estant, il n'y a plus moyen, ny d'esperance de le pouvoir r'allumer, bien que vos luy donniez l'huyle a regorger." (Paré, *Oeuvres,* p. 838)

See also *Batman vppon Bartholome,* fols. 98b–99b.

250: Beauty, that's colour, and proportion. The definition was probably originated by Plotinus, who rejected previous definitions concerned only with symmetry and added a new element:

Beauty is rather a light that plays over the symmetry of things than the symmetry itself, and in this consists its charm. For why is the light of beauty rather on the living face, and only a trace of it on that of the dead, though the countenance be not yet disfigured in the symmetry of its substance? (*Ennead,* IV, 7, 22)

Aquinas, however, had a different Platonist in mind: "sicut accipi potest ex verbis Dionysii, cap. 4 de div. Nom., (part. 1, lect. 5 et 6), ad rationem pulchri, sive decori, concurrit et claritas, et debita proportio. Dicit enim quod Deus dicitur *pulcher,* sicut *universorum consonantiae, et claritatis causa*" (*Summa,* II–II, Q. 145, a. 2). See also *Summa* II–II, Q. 180, a. 2; Augustine, *PL* 41, 781; *Batman vppon Bartholome,* fol. 390a.

253: perplexed. Either involuted, infolded, tangled (Latin *perplexus*) or confusing to the observer; but they are not mutually exclusive. It is the perplexity of the heavens that makes them perplexing; and throughout this section (lines 251–84) Donne shifts constantly from one to the other.

255: Eccentrique parts. An allusion to the eccentric circles of Ptolemaic astronomy used to make necessary adjustments in confused data. Cf. Milton, *Paradise Lost,* VIII, 75–84 and lines 275–77 below.

256: downe-right lines . . . ouerthwarts. Downe-right lines are lines directed straight downward. Ouerthwarts are transverse lines. But Donne may also have a pun in mind since downright has an overtone of directness, straightforwardness, whereas overthwart carries an additional meaning of oblique, askew, awry.

257–258. Grierson, following Norton, noted that Hipparchus was the first to divide the stars into forty-eight constellations, but that is not quite accurate. It was Ptolemy, in the tables (adapted from Hipparchus' catalogue) composing the seventh and eighth books of the *Almagest.* The lines tearing the firmament refer to those on an astronomical map of the heavens. Cf. Gregor Reisch, *Margarita Philosophica* (n. p., 1515, VII, i, 21): "Ex his firmamenti stellis astrologorum noñulli imagiñň quorñdā lineamēta imaginati sunt: non tamen credendum eas in celo realiter actu existere aut coloribus tineta q̄libus depingntur."

259–260. In 1572 Tycho Brahe discovered a new star in the constellation of Cassiopeia. In 1606 Kepler discovered two others, one in the Serpent on September 30, 1604, and the other in the Swan in the year 1600. And finally in 1610 Galileo announced in his *Siderius Nuncius* that he had discovered four satellites of Jupiter and an innumerable number of fixed stars. To most men of the time that meant that there was madness somewhere, either in the astronomers or in the sky itself. For according to the Ptolemaic system, the heavens were immutable, subject neither to generation nor corruption. See *The Second Anniversary,* lines 137–138 and notes. Cf. Burton (II, ii, 3) for the vortex of contemporary opinion; see also Hakewill, *An Apologie,* p. 81. In re-

ferring to the loss of old stars Donne has shifted his ground from
the disproportion observable in the sky to the disproportion
projected upon it by the confused notions of astronomers. According to Charles M. Coffin (*John Donne and the New Philosophy* [New York, 1938], p. 135), only 777 stars out of Hipparchus' 1022 were retained by Tycho Brahe in his famous
inventory of the heavenly bodies.

267: Tropiques. It is impossible to tell precisely how Donne
is using this word. He has apparently fused two somewhat different meanings. By having the Goat and Crab drive back the
sun from its attempted escapes to the poles, he obviously refers
to the two solstitial points, when the sun, entering the signs of
Capricorn and Cancer (December 12 and June 11 according to
the Julian calendar), reaches its maximum declination and
seems to turn back, that is, shift its ecliptic, decreasing its
obliquity. In the seventeenth century these solstitial points were
better known as *tropics.* By saying that these tropics fetter the
sun, however, Donne shifts his meaning to what I suppose he
would call the sun's two chains, the present tropics of Capricorn
and Cancer, north and south of the equator and parallel to it,
touching the ecliptic at the solstitial points.

268–272. According to Charles M. Coffin (*John Donne and
the New Philosophy,* p. 136) these lines refer to observed varia-
tions in the obliquity of the ecliptic. Since it seemed to decrease
throughout the ages, men were afraid that the declination would
eventually disappear, leaving the ecliptic constantly somewhere
about the equator. This was undoubtedly one of the great astronomical problems of the age. (See, for example, Hieronymus
Frascatorius, *Opera* [Venetiis, 1550], fol. 36b; Spenser, *FQ*, V,
vii; Hakewill, *An Apologie,* pp. 101–102; Alsted, II, 393). But
I do not believe that Donne is referring to it here. In fact, I
think he is saying the opposite; it is not that the sun is settling
down to a tame orbit near the equator, but that it is constantly
attempting to dash off to the poles. In other words, Donne is
simply talking about the constant shifts in the obliquity of

the ecliptic forming the procession of the equinoxes, fantasti-
cally proclaiming them proof of the sun's inability to "Perfit a
Circle."

271: cousening. Deceiving, sneaking, cheating.

273–274. Cf.

> [it is] an opinion of very *many*, and those very *learned* men, that the
> Body of the Sunne is drawne nearer the Earth by many degrees then
> it was in former ages, & that it daily makes descents & approaches
> towards it. . . . *Bodin* out of *Copernicus, Reinoldus* and *Stadius,*
> great Mathematicians tell vs, that since *Ptolomies* time . . . the
> *Sunne* by cleare demonstrations is found to haue come neerer vs
> by *one hundred & thirty semidiameters of the earth* [106, 640 Eng-
> lish miles]. . . . This wonderfull change, *Philip Melancthon*, saith
> he, *ad coelestium, terrestriumque corporum tabescentem naturam
> referendum putavit."* (Hakewill, *An Apologie,* p. 99)

The problem arose from a series of confused observations, all of
which were assumed to be correct. Ptolemy had observed that the
sun's distance from the earth was 1,210 semidiameters; Alba-
tegnius in 880 A.D. put it at 1,146, and from a series of such
mistakes men like Bodin drew the conclusion that the sun was
coming closer every year (Hakewill, p. 100). Not everyone, of
course, believed the statistics. Hakewill objects vehemently, and
J. C. Scaliger wrote that those who believed in it "vel ipsa scripta
spongiis, vel ipsa authores scuticis sunt castigandi"; in the margin
is the name *Copernicus* (*Exercitationes,* p. 343).

277: All their proportion's lame, it sinks, it swels. The image
is of a cripple, with one leg shorter than the other, alternately
rising and falling. For the basis of the image in Ptolemaic astronomy, cf. "stellis omnibus id videtur accidere, vt modo maiores,
& ppinquiores, modo minores, et remotiores videantur: cuius rei
multae tradûtur ab Astronomis causę . . . ; duobus autem

modis euenire dicunt . . . ; vno modo per vocatos ab ipsis Ecentricos orbes, alio per Epicyclos" (Frascatorius, *Opera*, fol. 17a). An eccentric was a seemingly lopsided planetary orbit, one in which the earth was not at the exact center, but dislocated; an epicycle was a small circle (described by a planet), the center of which moved along the eccentric.

His igitur duobus orbibus fieri dicunt, vt planeta modo altior, modo depressior sit: nam in Abside [the wide side, the bulge of the eccentric] quidam Ecētrici, & remotior à centro terrae, & sublimior sit, praesertim si & in summo Epicyclo sit: in Antabside [the narrow side of the eccentric] vero ppinquior redditur nobis, & magis si in imo Epicyclo extiterit: quae autem propinquiora, omnia & maiora apparent, quae vero remotiora minora simul videntur. (Frascatorius, fol. 17b)

For a more detailed explanation, see Edward Rosen, *Three Copernican Treatises* (New York, 1939), pp. 34–38.

278: Meridians, and Parallels. Loosely used as celestial longitude and latitude.

281–282. Cf. "*Quis ascendet,* says *David; who shall ascend unto the hill of the Lord?* It is a painfull clambring; up a hill" (*Sermons*, II, 135).

280: and now they are his owne. Because he has caught them with his net. As the metaphor becomes fully developed in lines 283–84, they turn out to be wild horses man has broken and now rides.

284: diuersly. Either that some are spurred and some are reined depending on how we want them to go or that some obey whereas others, not yet completely trained, ignore us. Either way, however, it ends up in a racing gallop.

285: But keepes the earth her round proportion still?   The argument from here to line 301 is an inversion of one of the most cherished *topoi* of Renaissance cosmographers:

> Qui igitur negant, terram globi figuram habere posse propter maris curvaturas et montium exsuperantias, inscite nugantur. Neque enim mons altior quam quindecim stadia ad perpendiculum reperitur, nec maris profunditas. Triginta autem stadia ad plus octoginta milia rationem nullam habent; quod non aliter se habet, si pulvisculus in pila esset. Atque tubercula, quae sunt in pilulis platanorum, non prohibent, quin sunt pilulae, quamquam illa ad totam pilulorum magnitudinem maiorem rationem habent quam curvaturae maris et montium exsuperantiae ad totam terrae magnitudinem.

To believe otherwise would destroy a perfect form: "Itaque omnino necesse est, etiam universum mundum hac figura uti. Atque re vera etiam illud maxime credibile est, perfectissimum corpus perfectissima uti figura. Atque est omnium corporum perfectissimum mundus, omnium figurarum sphaera" (Cleomedes, *De Motu Circulari Corpori Caelestium,* ed. and trans. Hermannus Ziegler [Lipsiae, 1891], pp. 103, 87; for Renaissance restatements see Sebastian Munster, *Cosmographiae Universalis* [Basileae, 1554], pp. 11–12; Alsted, II, 529; Gilbert, *De Magnete,* pp. 65, 339; and Burton, II, ii, 3). Donne's argument consists primarily of what logicians would call a reproof; he answers the *topos* point by point. But the argument itself is basically Medieval. Pseudo-Bede (*PL* 93, 222), Rabanus Maurus (*PL* 107, 519), and Petrus Comestor (*PL* 198, 1084) had all implied that the face of the earth is foul because of original sin.

286–294.   Cf. Burton, II, ii, 3: "The pike of Teneriff how high is it? 79 miles, or 52, as Patricius holds, or 9 as Snellius demonstrates in his Eratosthenes"? He would also like to know

> Whether Mount Athos, Pelion, Olympus, Ossa, Caucasus, Atlas, be so high as Pliny, Solinus, Mela relate, above clouds, meteors, *ubi nec aurae nec venti spirant* . . . , 1250 paces high, according to that

measure of Dicaearchus, or 78 miles perpendicularly high, as Jacobus
Mazonius . . . and as Blancanus the Jesuite contends . . . ; or
rather 32 stadiums, as the most received opinion is; or 4 miles, which
the height of no mountain doth perpendicularly exceed, and is equal
to the greatest depths of the sea, which is, as Scaliger holds, 1580
paces . . . , others 100 paces.

289–291. Cf. Ulysses Aldrovandus (*De Piscibus* [Bononiae,
1638], p. 673): after trying in vain to shake the hook (usually
baited with a whole ox liver), whales finally sound: "acerrimis
doloribus affecta, in pelagi profundum demergitur. . . . Cum
autem peruenit ad imam maris sedem, defatigata quiescit, ingentes
fluctus anhelans."

292–294. Cf. *As You Like It*, IV, i, 211–212: "My affection
hath an unknown bottom, like the bay of Portugal." Donne
seems to retain the fishing image, implying that with all that
line out it is almost as though they were fishing for antipodes,
people on the other side of the world, whose feet are planted
opposite ours (ἀντί + πόδες). Belief in the antipodes had been
attacked by the Church Fathers, but after the explorations of the
Renaissance, it came back into being again. See Josephus Isaeus'
notes in his edition of Lactantius (Caeserae, 1616), reprinted in
PL 6, 426; Hakewill, *An Apologie*, p. 249.

295–299. Cf.

one Author, who is afraid of admitting too great a hollownesse in
the Earth, lest then the Earth might not be said to be solid, pro-
nounces that Hell cannot possibly be above three thousand miles in
compasse, (and then one of the torments of Hell will be the throng,
for their bodies [reassumed in the general resurrection] must be
there, in their dimensions, as well as their soules). (*Sermons*, VII,
137)

A marginal note identifies the author as Sebastian Munster, who
wrote: "Est quidē magna cauerna, capax tot milliū corporum

humanorū damnatorū, sed quae nihil est, ut diximus collata ad terrā, etiamsi longitudine & latitudine atq; altitudine duo aut tria millia contineat Germanicorū miliariorū" (*Cosmographiae Universalis* [Basileae, 1554], p. 11–12). Donne was not the only one distressed by Munster and his shrunken hell; Antonio Rusca, the foremost Renaissance authority on hell, considered him completely unreasonable: "Minùs fortè id improbabile, quamquàm sine fundamento rationis" (*De Inferno* [Mediolani, 1621], p. 169; see also pp. 164–66). But actually Munster's estimate was modest compared with some others. Franciscus Ribera allowed hell a diameter of only 200 Italian miles, and Lessius reduced it to one Dutch mile "all filled with fire and brimstone; because . . . that space, cubically multiplied, will make a sphere able to hold eight hundred thousand millions of damned bodies (allowing each body six foot square)" (Burton, II, ii, 3).

300–301.   Cf. Cleomedes' "pulvisculus in pila" and "tubercula, quae sunt in pilulis platanorum" in the notes to line 285; cf. also Gilbert, *De Magnete*, p. 339. Donne's argument goes something like this: after I have just proved the opposite of what you say by showing you mountains that reach the moon, seas that pierce straight through the earth, and the resulting vacancy reduced to void by the hollowness of the middle, do you still contend as before that these are only minor excrescences? No matter. But yet grant me this. . . .

311: *that Ancient*.   Grosart and Chambers suggest Pythagoras; Norton suggests Simmias in Plato's *Phaedo*; Grierson suggests Aristoxenus, primarily because Cicero (*Tusc. Disp.*, I, 10) and Burton (I, i, 2) both associated him with the idea of the soul as harmony. As Grierson's discussion makes clear, however, there were a number of others who believed the same thing: "Two classes of thinkers . . . regarded the soul as a harmony, doctors as Hippocrates and Galen, who considered it a harmony of the four elements . . . ; and musicians like Aristoxenus, who compared the soul to the harmony of the lyre." Cf. Plato, *Timaeus*, 43d and Eryximachus' definition of love in the *Symposium*;

Aristotle, *De Anima*, 407b 27–33. With so many possibilities, I doubt that Donne's vague reference can be identified with any certainty.

312: at next. As Grierson noted, this common Old English construction seems to have been very rare in Donne's time. The *OED* cites no use later than Pecock's *Repression* in 1449: "Immediatli at next to the now before alleggid text of Peter this proces folewith."

314: Resultances. The *OED* uses this as one of its three citations exemplifying "Something which issues, proceeds, or emanates from another thing."

316: As to our eyes, the formes from obiects flow. This theory of vision is usually associated with the Epicureans. Cf. A. Wolf, *A History of Science* (London, 1935), p. 244 and Cyril Bailey's commentary in his monumental edition of Lucretius (Oxford, 1947), III, 1179–81. In the Renaissance, however, it was regarded as Aristotelian (*De Sensu et Sensibili*, 437a–438b) and in general was the most commonly received opinion:

> Aristoteles, princeps Peripati, & princeps Opticorum Alhazenus & Vitello docent, visionem fieri . . . *immissiuè*. Euclides, Stoici, Ptolemaeus, & Galenus putant, visionem fieri . . . *emissuè*, ita vt radij ab oculis emittantur ad obiecta. Pythagoras denique & Plato putant fieri . . . per corradiationem, ita vt radij partim emittantur, partim recipiantur. . . . Ex his tribus sententiis sola prima vera est. (Alsted, II, 603)

See also *Batman vppon Bartholome*, fol. 389b.

317–319. Probably Ambrose (*PL* 14, 387–88) and Augustine (*PL* 41, 472). Although both make generally the same point, they differ in their mathematical equations and the applications of their discussions. Ambrose presents an extensive allegory similar to Spenser's House of Alma: man is an isolated figure surrounded and almost overwhelmed by a flood of cupidity. Augustine on the other hand takes the ark as a type of the church, built in the proportions of Christ, who saved us from the deluge of sin.

319–322. Cf.

> in the *Arke* there were Lions, but the Lion shut his mouth, and clincht his paw, (the Lion hurt nothing in the Arke) and in the Arke there were Vipers and Scorpions, but the Viper shewed no teeth, nor the Scorpion no taile, (the Viper bit none, the Scorpion stung none in the Arke) (for, if they had occasioned any disorder there, their escape could have been but into the Sea, into irreparable ruine).
> (*Sermons*, III, 184)

For similar allusions see D. C. Allen, *The Legend of Noah* (Urbana, Ill., 1949), pp. 77, 148, who cites John Lightfoot, David Pareus, Skelton, Cowley, Herrick, Flatman, Quarles, and Marvell. The use of the ark as a type of the just man's inner peace was traditional. Cf. Ambrose: "Quis est justus in nobis, nisi mentis vigor qui intra istam arcam includat omne animantium genus, quod est super terram. Cohibe ergo et tu omnes irrationabiles passiones tuas, omnesque sensus tuos menti subjice, animique imperiis assuesce" (*PL* 14, 394).

329–338. Donne shifts from the inner proportion in the mind and heart of a just man to the manifestation of that proportion in the decorous, harmonious actions of his daily life. Lines 332–338 are particularly difficult: if wise and good observers are not satisfied with the performance of our actions, then the actions as well as their sources are undoubtedly loathsome and deformed because almost all men are exactly what the majority of men think they are. Cf.

> for the most part, most men are such, as most men take them to be; *Neminem omnes, nemo omnes fefellit:* All the world never joyned to deceive one man, nor was ever any one man able to deceive all the world. *Contemptu famae contemnuntur & virtutes,* was so well said by *Tacitus,* as it is pity S. *Augustine* said it not, They that neg-

lect the good opinion of others, neglect those vertues that should produce that good opinion. (*Sermons*, VIII, 323)

See also *Sermons*, VI, 155. The last two lines (337–38) recapitulate the entire section: the inner source of our actions (*good*) and the outward performance of those actions (*well*) must harmonize, for wickedness is not much worse than its outward manifestation, indiscreetness.

343–344. Believed to be a common property of turquoise. Anselmus Boethius de Boot, for example, tells of a ring his father bought him at an auction in Spain. The stone had lost its color, but as soon as he wore it for a few months, all its former beauty miraculously returned:

> Mutatio coloris naturaliter fieri potest. Nam cum non adeo dura sit gemma facile à vapore, & halitu qui per poros cutis perpetuo transpirant, vel pulchrum, vel absurdum, & deformem colorem accipere potest. . . . Animadverti, cum icteritia, vel obstructionibus laborassem, & iam corpus sudoribus transpirabile, ac bene constitutum esset, meam Turcoidem pulchriorem esse, ita ut mihi valetudinis index sit. (*Gemmarum et Lapidum Historia*, ed. Adrianus Toll [Lugduni Batavorum, 1636], pp. 266–69)

See also Ulysses Aldrovandus, *Musaeum Metallicum* (Bononiae, 1648), p. 902; Andreas Baccius, *De Gemmis et Lapidibus Pretiosis*, trans. Wolfgangus Gabelchoverus (Francofurti, 1603), pp. 168–70.

345: As gold fals sicke being stung with Mercury. Gold amalgam is an extremely common alloy; with thirteen percent or more gold present it consists of yellowish-white crystals. For a Renaissance description of the process, cf.

> in amicitiam auri [Hydrargyrum, *i.e.*, Mercurius] abundè incidit, quia illius sordes mirandum in modum abstergit; illique adeò ad-

haerit vt auri substantiam citò penetret, illudque fragilius oui cortice reddat; propterea annuli aurei dealbantur, si gestantes per loca transierint, in quibus Hydrargyrum elaboratur; quod sibi pluries contigisse Cardanus narrat. Cuncta igitur metalla Hydrargyro supernatant, vno excepto auro, quod Argento viuo impositum statim ab eo absorbetur. (Ulysses Aldrovandus, *Musaeum Metallicum* [Bononiae, 1648], p. 197)

See also Aldrovandus, pp. 194–201; Alsted, I, 150–51; Scaliger, *Exercitationes*, p. 323.

352: *Himselfe his various Rainbow did allow.* An allusion to the traditional controversy whether the rainbow existed before the Deluge, when God told Noah that He would put His bow in the sky as a token of their new covenant (Genesis 9:11–17). Medieval exegetes, such as Alcuin (*PL* 100, 532), thought that since there was no rain before the Flood, there was no rainbow either. By the Renaissance, however, it was agreed that rainbows had always existed, but that they had no meaning until God made them a sign of His mercy and peace: "Negant quidam Iridem fuisse ante illud tempus: Verùm textus Hebraeus indicat etiam antè fuisse, sed tum primum signum foederis esse coepit, quod diluvium ampliùs non esset venturum" (Sebastian Munster, cited in *Critici Sacri*, I, 155). See also pp. 159, 160, for almost identical statements by Paulus Fagius and Sebastian Castalio; *Essays in Divinity*, pp. 88–89; Pererius, pp. 134–35; John Diodati, *Pious Annotations upon the Holy Bible* (London, 1648), p. 89; á Lapide, *Commentaria in Pentateuchum*, pp. 126–27.

353: *Sight is the noblest sense of any one.* Cf.

Visus omnium sensuum externorum est praestantissimus. Nam hic solus totum obiectum, & omnes eius partes percipit: solus miram obiectorum varietatem dignoscit: non impeditur contrariis: menti est quàm simillimus: ad capessendum disciplinas est vtilissimus: est sensum externorum velocissimus: homini dilectissimus: habet organum pulcherrimum & artificiosissimum. (Alsted, II, 166)

See also Aquinas, *Summa*, I, Q. 67, a. 1 and *Commentum in Quatuor Libros Sententiarum*, I, d. xvii, q. 1, a. 1; Gregor Reisch, *Margarita Philosophica* (n. p., 1515), X, ii, 6; *Batman vppon Bartholome*, fol. 18b; Paré, *Oeuvres*, p. 120; *Sermons*, VIII, 221.

354: Sight hath onely color to feed on. Donne has in mind Aristotle's definition of color:

> the Translucent, according to the degree to which it subsists in bodies (and it does so in all more or less), . . . causes them to partake of color. But since the color is at the extremity of the body, it must be at the extremity of the Translucent in the body. Whence it follows that we may define colour as the limit of the Translucent in determinately bounded body. (*De Sensu et Sensibili*, 439b 9–13).

Since color was nothing less than the entire surface of the body, it necessarily included form: "Sublato verò colore, omnem in mundo visionem interire necesse est; cum omne visibile non nisi per superficiem coloratam spectetur" (Athanasius Kircher, *Ars Magna Lucis et Umbrae* [Amstelodami, 1671], p. 47; Kircher, p. 48, has an excellent commentary on Aristotle's definition; see also *Batman vppon Bartholome*, fol. 384b; Alsted, II, 166; *Biathanatos*, p. 154).

357–358. Besides indicating a state of innocence, the "blushing redde" is something like a pun in Hebrew. Cf. "Another name of man is *Adam*, and *Adam* is no more but *earth*, and *red earth*, and the word is often used for *blushing*" (*Sermons*, X, 197; see also II, 78–79, 200). What Donne means is that there is no difference between the words *Adam* and *blush* in Hebrew written without vowel points, and even with the points, there is only a slight distinction: אָדַם = *blush*; אָדָם = *Adam*. For a paraphrase of the entire image, cf:

> He made us all of earth, and all of red earth. Our earth was red, even when it was in Gods hands: a rednesse that amounts to a

shamefastnesse, to a blushing at our own infirmities, is imprinted in us, by Gods hand. . . . But that redness, which we have contracted from bloud shed by our selves, the bloud of our own souls, by sinne, was not upon us, when we were in the hands of God. . . . Our sinnes are our owne, and our destruction is from our selves. . . . We have dyed our selves in sinnes, as red as Scarlet [Isaiah 1:18]. (*Sermons*, IX, 64–66)

361–363. Besides the white and red of her complexion and the blue of her eyes "(Beauties ingredients)," the colors are also those of the theological virtues, which explains why they constitute "an vnuext Paradise." Although green was usually used for hope (Dante, *Purgatorio*, XXX, 31–33; Cesare Ripa, *Iconologia* [Venetia, 1669], p. 589), blue was a recognized variant: "Hyacinthus quoniam aeris et coeli speciem imitatur, eorumdem mentes electorum omni spe et desiderio coelestia quaerentes significat" (Rabanus Maurus, *PL* 111, 579; see also Spenser, *FQ*, I, x, 14).

364: verdure. The fresh green of new vegetation.

365–366. The important word is *miraculous.* Only the white light of eternity was believed to be all diaphanous, not stained into color by earth's shadows:

> Certum est nullum in hoc sublunaris mundi ambitu corpus adeo diaphanum, quod non quamdam sibi adjunctam habeat ocacitatem, reperiri; unde consequenter si nullum foret in hoc mundo opacum, neque luminis reflexio, aut in diversis mediis eiusdem refractio, nullum quoque in mundo colorem praeterquam primigenium illum luci concreatum, conspicuum futurum certum est . . . ; imò ne lucidum quidem Solis corpus videri posset, nisi id opacum esset, & visum nostrum sisteret. (Athanasius Kircher, *Ars Magna Lucis et Umbrae* [Amstelodami, 1671], p. 47)

See also Aquinas, *Commentaria in Aristotelis De Anima*, II, xiv; *Biblia latina, cum postillis Nicolai de Lyra et additionibus Pauli*

Burgensis (Nuremberg, 1497), I, fol. 26a; *Sermons*, III, 355.
Since celestial light was the source of all color, however, it contained all color in potential.

378: her influence. The influence of Donne's symbolic she as
indentified and equated with the influence of the stars.

380: The father, or the mother barren is. The mother is traditionally the passive, receptive earth, and the father, the sky:

> Denique caelesti sumus semine oriundi;
> omnibus ille idem pater est, unde alma liquentis
> umoris guttas mater cum terra recepit,
> feta parit nitidas fruges . . .
>
> .   .   .   .
>
> quapropter merito maternum nomen adepta est.
> (Lucretius, *De Rerum Natura*, II, 991–94, 998)

In general the same is true here, but in the next few lines it
becomes more complicated: although the elements above the
earth are female to impressions from beyond the sphere of the
moon, they are not entirely passive; they also work on the earth
below them, either masculinely, like clouds, or femininely, like
air.

387–388. In the Renaissance the word *meteor* referred to any
atmospheric phenomenon—snow, rain, lightning, dew, rainbows,
wind. It was commonly believed that important events were
forecast by prodigious happenings, such as the "exhalations
whipping in the air" and the "portentous things" in Act I, scene
iii of *Julius Caesar*. But it was also believed that the heavens
were increasingly subject to monstrous abortions: it not only
rained stones "sed & lacte, lana ac sanguine, annona, manna,
adipe ac piscibus, sed & cinere, atque etiam muribus, & coturni-
cibus, ac sagittis, & carnibus" (Simon Maiolus, *Dies Caniculares*
[Moguntiae, 1607], p. 26; see Burton, II, ii, 3, for a parallel,
somewhat more extended catalogue). Conrad Lycosthenes wrote

the standard book on the subject, a year by year almost day by day catalogue of incomprehensible meteorological disturbances entitled *Prodigiorum ac Ostentorum Chronicon* (Basileae, 1577). See also Ulysses Aldrovandus, *Monstrorum Historia* (Bononiae, 1642), pp. 721–33.

389–390: new wormes. A pun fusing tenor and vehicle. In the image they are maggots bred from the decay of a rotten world, but in the vehicle they are snakes (a common use of the word *worm* in the seventeenth century), specifically, the new species discovered in Africa and America (Maiolus, *Dies Caniculares*, p. 303). According to Renaissance herpetologists (and this is probably the fact that permitted Donne's metaphor) snakes were also bred from corruption:

Alij ex terra, seu potius ex putredine terrae Serpentes prodijsse, hacque ratione Pythonem magnum illum Serpentem olim progenitum fuisse litteris demandarunt. . . . Ouidius hunc Serpentis ortum eleganter diuulgat his versibus:

> Ergo ubi diluuio tellus, lutulenta recenti
> Solibus aethereis, altoq; recanduit aestu;
> *Edidit innumeras species, partimq; figuras*
> *Reddidit antiquas: partim noua monstra creauit.*
> Illa quidem nollet, sed te quoq; maxime Python
> Tum genuit, populisq; nouis incognite Serpens
> Terror eras.   [*Meta.*, I, 434–40; the italics are mine.]

. . . Verū postquam verba fiunt de ortu Serpentum ex putridis prodeunte, non erit ab re praedictis addere eorū opinionem, qui ex putrescentibus humanis carnibus, vel potius ex corrupta spinae medulla Serpentes generari asseruerunt.

Vergil (*Aeneid*, V, 90–99) and Paré (*Oeuvres*, p. 664) offer conclusive evidence. "Non esse igitur prodigiosum ex humano cadauere Serpentis ortum credendum est. . . . [Sed] multò magis ex terra, & imbre putrescentibus Serpentes progigni potuerunt" (Ulysses Aldrovandus, *Serpentum, et Draconū*

Historiae [Bononiae, 1640], pp. 15–16; see also Scaliger, *Exercitationes,* pp. 627–28).

390: Th'Egyptian Mages. Exodus 7:10–12:

And Moses and Aaron went in unto Pharaoh, and they did so as the Lord commanded: and Aaron cast down his rod before Pharaoh, and before his servants, and it became a serpent. Then Pharaoh also called the wise men and the sorcerers: now the magicians of Egypt, they also did in like manner with their enchantments. For they cast down every man his rod, and they became serpents: but Aaron's rod swallowed up their rods.

391–396. Cf.

As to cure diseases by touch, or by charme, (both which one excellent Chirugian, and one excellent philosopher, are of opinion may be done, because what vertue soever the heavens infuse into any creature, man who is Al, is capable of, and being borne when that vertue is exacted, may receive a like impression, or may give it to a word, or character made at that instant, if he can understand the time) though these, I say be forbidden by divers Lawes, out of a just prejudice that vulgar owners of such a vertue, would mis-imploy, it, yet none mislikes that the Kings of *England* & *France,* should cure our sicknesse by such meanes. (*Biathanatos,* pp. 216–17)

A marginal note identifies the "excellent Chirugian" as Paracelsus, who urged physicians to rediscover the lost astromedical techniques of the Medes and Persians:

Artes quaedam chirurgicae, à primis Astronomiae cultoribus inuentae sunt, quibus admiranda (virtute aetherea) in vulneribus praestabant. Verum eae post obitum antiquorum Magorum sic deperditae sunt, vt vix aliqua vestigia supersint amplius. Ars autem coelestium impressionum erat, vt actionem influentem in corpoream aliquam substantiam deducerent, in qua deinde vigeret. . . . Opera igitur danda est Chirurgo, vt vires Gemmarum, herbarum, Radicum, ac seminum

coelitus infusas accurate cognoscat: nec horum solum, sed &
characterum ac verborum quoque. (*Opera*, III, 22)

By flatly stating that this art is now completely and forever lost
because of the weakening influence of the stars and the increasing
feebleness of man's mind, Donne hoisted Paracelsus on his own
petard.

391: Artist. One who deals in occult arts, in this case an
astrologer.

402: worke. In the sense of an operative power or efficacy,
somewhat ambivalently identified with the influence of the stars.
As the image unfolds in the next twelve lines, we find ourselves
exploring with Donne the complexities of the word *vertue*, attempting to comprehend through similar metaphors involving
the occult working of physical powers her unseen, spiritual influence.

404: Ashes too, are medicinall. The ashes of certain herbs were
prescribed for the treatment of specific diseases. Cf. "Cinis omnis
ustione igneas partes conquirit: ficulneus valide extenuat &
absumit, acrimoniae urentisque facultalibus plurimum sortitus.
Huic proximus est sarmentitus & qui ex ilice aut brassica sumitur.
Omnes cum axungia vel oles illiti oldemata discutiunt, articu-
lorum doloribus, nervorum nodis & contusionibus mire prosunt"
(Ferelius, cited by Allen, "Renaissance Medicine," p. 340). The
ashes of snakes were also used, particularly for toothaches and
boils (Ulysses Aldrovandus, *Serpentum, et Draconŭ Historiae*
[Bononiae, 1640], p. 104).

407–408. Plato supplies the best gloss, not so much the
facts, which are ubiquitous in Western literature, but for the extension of the image and the tone. Just before Socrates drinks
the hemlock, he tries to persuade his friends that he is not mis-
fortunate:

Will you not allow that I have as much of the spirit of prophecy in me as the swans? For they, when they perceive that they must die, having sung all their life long, do then sing more lustily than ever, rejoicing in the thought that they are about to go away to the god whose ministers they are. . . . But because they are sacred to Apollo, they have the gift of prophecy, and anticipate the good things of another world; wherefore they sing and rejoice in that day more than ever they did before. (*Phaedo*, 84e)

See also Cicero, *Tusc. Disp.*, I, xxx, 73; Ovid, *Heroides*, VII; Pliny, *Nat. Hist.*, X, 32.

409–412. Cf "there are diuers poysons which cannot work, except they be eiaculated from the creature it selfe that possesseth it, and that his personall and present liuely malignity concurre to it, and giue it vigour" (*Pseudo-Martyr*, pp. 140–41; see also Gosse, *Life and Letters*, I, 122). This was not common knowledge; none of the Renaissance authorities on poisons—Matthioli, Paré, Topsell, Aldrovandus—mentions it, at least not exactly as Donne has it. Paré, for example, notes in passing that the natural warmth of living animals makes their poisons more lethal (*Oeuvres*, p. 487). And Aldrovandus explains that some people think the malignity of a serpent increases the effect of its poison: "nam in illa actione, bilis subtilissima per totum corpus disseminatur, consequenterq; portio biliosa circa dentes in morsu relinquitur; haec autem quo potentior est, eò velocius partem demorsam corrumpit, illamq; in sui naturam vertit; atq; ita venenum augetur; quemadmodum ignis materiam comburendo crescit." But Aldrovandus himself did not believe that, since he knew that snakes had very little bile (*Serpentum, et Draconu Historiae*, p. 91). Donne may have gotten his information from van Forrest's *De Venenis*, which he mentions a number of times in *Pseudo-Martyr* and which was not available to me.

421–422. Some people have some restraint and crave no more than Kings should give them.

424: graines.   The least amount possible; a figurative use of the smallest contemporary unit of weight, a grain of dried wheat.

431–434.   Cf. I Peter 1:2–4:

> Grace and peace be multiplied unto you through the knowledge of God, and of Jesus our Lord, According as his divine power hath given unto us all things that pertain unto life and godliness, through the knowledge of him that hath called us to glory and virtue: Whereby are given unto us exceeding great and precious promises: that by these ye might be partakers of the divine nature, having escaped the corruption that is in the world through lust.

Throughout his life this text was extremely important to Donne. He returned to it often in his sermons. Cf.

> we are made partakers of the divine nature . . . ; not that we are so derived from the nature and essence of God, as that our souls should be of his very substance . . . , But this transmutation is a glorious restoring of Gods image in us . . . which admits no re-transmutation . . . ; for as a spirit cannot be divided, so they who are thus changed into him, are so much His, so much He, that nothing can separate them from him; and this is the ladder, by which we may try, how far we are in the way to heaven. (*Sermons*, I, 164)

See also *Sermons*, III, 113, 224; I Corinthians 6:17–19.

440: punctuall.   Minute, detailed, dealing with the matter thoroughly point by point.

446: Whose name refines course lines, and makes prose song. Simply by having your name in them, the lines assume value. But at the same time Donne implies the mysterious name at the beginning of the poem, lines 31–38.

447: rent.   Cf. "since God hath made us his *Tenants* of this World, we are bound . . . to pay our *Rents*, (*spiritual* duties and services towards him)" (*Sermons,* I, 222). In a later sermon Donne tells us to "pay God his rent of praise and prayer" since we are living in his country house on the outskirts of the heavenly Jerusalem (III, 288).

449–451.   Cf. the ecclesiastical meaning of *anniversary* in notes above to title. Cf. also "the Primitive Church . . . called the Martyrs dayes, wherein they suffered, *Natalitia Martyrum,* their birth dayes" (*Sermons,* II, 200).

456: concoction.   Refined, purified, brought to a state of perfection; usually applied to the maturation of gold or gems in the earth by the slow heat of the sun. Cf.

> Precious stones are first *drops of the dew* of heaven, and then refined by the sunne of heaven. When by long lying they have exhal'd, and evaporated, and breathed out all their grosse matter, and received another concoction from the sunne, then they become precious, in the eye, and estimation of men. (*Sermons,* III, 372)

See also *Sermons,* I, 272; "The Extasie," 21–28; Martinus Del Rio, *Disquisitionum Magicarum Libri Sex* (Coloniae Agrippinae, 1676), pp. 70–71.

461–466.   Cf. Deuteronomy 31–33. Just before the Israelites were to enter the Promised Land, the Lord spoke to Moses and Joshua from a pillar of cloud and told them that the people would forsake Him: "Now therefore write ye this song for you, and teach it the children of Israel: put it in their mouths, that this song may be a witness for me against the children of Israel" (31:19). So Moses called the people together and taught them the words of God's song:

> . . . And he said, I will hide my face from them. . . . I will heap mischiefs upon them: I will spend mine arrows upon them. . . . For they are a nation void of counsel, neither is there any understanding in them. O that they were wise, that they understood this, that they

would consider their latter end. . . . See now that I, even I, am he, and there is no god with me: I kill, and I make alive; I wound and I heal: neither is there any that can deliver out of my hand. (30:20, 23, 28–29, 39)

Donne's gloss for the song, which he presents in these lines and throughout his works, is taken from John Chrysostom's *Interpretatio in Isaiam Prophetam*:

> Cur ergo criminationes ut canticum concinnant? Sapientia certe usi spirituali, et multum emolumenti auditorum animis inferre volentes. Quia enim nihil sic utile est, ut scelerum assidue recordari, nihilque memoriam ita firmam parit, et assiduam peccatorum memoriam subterfugerent, cantici modulatione pudorem subripiens ex memoria partum, et intolerabilem moerorem leniens, haec cantica fecit, ut melodiae amore coacti ad ea frequenter pronuntianda, saepe illorum recordarentur, assidueque doctrinam de colenda virtute haberent, nempe assiduam peccatorum recordationem. (*PG* 56, 57)

See also à Lapide, *Commentaria in Pentateuchum*, p. 1030; *Biathanatos*, p. 159; *Essays in Divinity*, p. 92. The song itself was regarded as a complete summary of the old dispensation, the Law, as opposed to the new, which began with the advent of Christ: "Dicunt Hebraei canticum istud esse . . . *summarium totius Legis*. Nam fecit mentionem de Magnificentia Dei, de Creatione mundi, de uno Deo colendo, de generatione Diluvii, de Divisione linguarum & terrarum, de electione populi Israelitici, de beneficio in deserto ei exhibito" (Sebastian Munster, cited in *Critici Sacri*, p. 1351; see also pp. 1354, 1355, 1361 for identical statements by Paulus Fagius, Franciscus Vetablus, and Isidorus Clarius). This was the standard gloss in the seventeenth century; see, for example, *Sermons*, II, 171; *Biathanatos*, p. 159; à Lapide, *Commentaria in Pentateuchum*, p. 1021; John Diodati, *Pious Annotations* (London, 1648), p. 111. Cf. Milton, *Paradise Lost*, XII, 300–303, 307–14:

> So Law appears imperfet, and but giv'n
> With purpose to resign them in full time

Up to a better Cov'nant, disciplin'd
From shadowy Types to Truth, from Flesh to Spirit . . .
And therefore shall not *Moses*, though of God
Highly belov'd, being but the Minister
Of Law, his people into *Canaan* lead;
But *Joshua* whom the Gentiles *Jesus* call,
His Name and Office bearing, who shall quell
The adversary Serpent, and bring back
Through the world's wilderness long wander'd man
Safe to eternal Paradise of rest.

474: fame. Grierson did not record the variant, *same*, even though Grosart had noted cryptically that "in a copy of the 1612 edition now before me, Donne (I think) has himself written 'fame,' lest the long *s*, so like an *f*, should be mistaken." Grosart had before him the Huth-Hagen-Chew-Harmsworth copy (now at the Folger Shakespeare Library), in which someone corrected a few obvious misprints.

A FUNERALL ELEGIE

Typographical note. All editions before 1633 indent every other line to give the impression of elegiac couplets.

1–21. A complex inversion of the topos *Exegi monumentum aere perennius* (Horace, *Odes*, III, 30). Cf. Propertius:

Nam neque Pyramidum sumptus ad sidera ducti,
    Nec Jovis Elei coelum imitata domus,
Nec Mausolei dives fortuna sepulcri,
    Mortis ab extrema conditione vacat.
Aut illis flamma, aut imber subducet honores,
    Annorum aut ictu pondera victa ruent.
At non ingenio quaesitum nomen ab aevo
    Excidet: ingenio stat sine morte decus.

                    (III, ii, 17–24)

See also Ovid, *Amores*, I, x, 61–62. Du Bellay, however, offers the best gloss. Like Donne, he knew that paper does not last:

Esperez vous que la posterité
  Doiue (mes vers) pour tout iamais vous lire?
  Esperez vous que l'oeuvre d'vne lyre
  Puisse acqueir telle immortalité?
Si sous le ciel fust quelque eternité,
  Les monuments que ie vous ay fait dire,
  Non en papier, mais en marbre et porphyre,
  Eussent gardé leur viue antiquité.
                    (*Antiquitez de Rome*, XXXII, 1–8)

8: ten escurials.   The Escorial, recently completed when these
lines were written, was one of the most lavish buildings of its age.
It was at once the residence and the mausoleum of Spanish kings.
Beneath the altar of the royal chapel, in what was called the
Pantheon, twenty black marble sarcophagi were reserved for future monarchs or their mothers. Other members of the royal
family were sealed in the *Pantheon de los Infantes,* delicately
known as *El Pudridero.* For meditations on worldly vanity nothing could be better; cf. "In the same Escurial, where the Spanish
princes live in greatness and power, and decree war or peace,
they have wisely placed a cemetery, where their ashes shall sleep
till time shall be no more" (Jeremy Taylor, *Holy Dying* in
Works, ed. R. Herber [London, 1839], IV, 344).

16: Tabernacle.   The word is exact; cf. "his most glorious
Creatures are but *vehicula Dei;* they are but chariots, which
convey God, and bring him to our sight; The *Tabernacle* it selfe
was but a *Mobilis domus,* and *Ecclesia portatilis,* a house without
a foundation; a running, a progresse house" (*Sermons,* II, 221;
see also 217).

27: spirits.   Both the delicate inspirations of music and the
spirits of the body, which unite body and soul. *Organ* in line 28
is also a pun, incorporating both areas of meaning.

27: tune and set.   An obsolete phrase meaning simply tune. It
still survives in the phrase to set in tune.

28: peeces. Both musical compositions (a piece of music) and distinguished individuals. Cf. line 71 below.

41–44. Until the nineteenth century, the Niger was associated with the upper waters of the Nile, and the attributes of one were often transferred to the other. Pliny, for example, explains that the Nile starts in a lake in Western Mauretania and proceeds underground until it approaches Ethiopia, "atque ubi iterum senserit hominem, prosilit, fonte (ut verisimile est) illo quem Nigrim vocavere" (*Nat. Hist.,* V, 10). Solinus identified the fountain with the river: "contingat Aethiopas, ubi exit et Nigrim facit fluvium, Astapum eum indigetes vocant, scilicet aquam e tenebris profluentem" (*Collectanea Rerum Memorabilium,* XXXII, 2–5; XXX, 1). Claudius Salmasius, however, Solinus' magnificent Renaissance editor, objected strongly to the identification and amended the text to read father (*patrem*) instead of part (*partem*) of the Nile (Trajecti ad Rhenum, 1689, I, 272, 297). Gerardus Mercator, on the other hand, followed Ptolemy's *Geography,* which followed Solinus, and located the headwaters of the Niger in the far west, near the Atlantic Ocean. It flowed directly east, sometimes above ground, sometimes below, until it finally joined the Nile and helped produce Egypt's annual flood (*Cl. Ptolemaei Alexandrini Geographiae Libri Octo* [Coloniae Agrippinae, 1584], fol. Na).

49–51. What is it to us if an Angel, a member of the lowest of the nine angelic orders, is promoted to the top of the hierarchy, either as a Throne (seventh) or a Cherub (eighth)? We lose by it because only the lower orders are concerned with man and his doings; Thrones and Cherubim stand transfixed in the contemplation of God. Cf. Aquinas, *Summa,* I, Q. 113, a. 3: "Utrum custodire homines pertineat solum ad infimum ordinem Angelorum" and I, Q. 112, a. 2: "Utrum omnes Angeli in ministerium mittantur." Most of Aquinas' information was derived from Pseudo-Dionysius, *De Coelesti Hierarchia,* VI–VII.

68: Artist. Used ironically for astronomers. The term usually referred to scientific quacks. Cf. *The First Anniversary*, line 391.

73–74. Balsamum was worth twice its weight in silver (Pliny, *Nat. Hist.*, XII, 54, 25). It was therefore not often used in lamps. Besides Donne only two other people in history seem to have thought of burning it. One was the Emperor Heliogobalus, who among his other excesses is said to have exhibited (*exhibuit*) balsamum in lamps (Lampridius, XXIV, 1). The other was Constantine the Great, who burned it for the honor and glory of God (*PL* 8, 803–804; see also *PL* 127, 1515–17; *Sermons*, IX, 152). Cf. Dryden's paraphrase:

> As precious gums are not for lasting fire,
> They but perfume the temple, and expire;
> So was she soon exhal'd, and vanished hence,
> A short sweet odour, of a vast expense.
> (Eleonora, 301–304)

81–82. Cf.

> I will finde out another death, *mortem raptus,* a death of rapture, and of extasie, that death which S. *Paul* died more then once, The death which S. *Gregory* speaks of, *Divina contemplatio quoddam sepulchrum animae,* The contemplation of God, and heaven, is a kinde of buriall, and Sepulchre, and rest of the soule. (*Sermons*, II, 210)

83: sad History. Although the 1611 text clearly reads *sad,* Grierson believed that it was not to be found in any early edition. He therefore printed *said,* but only under protest, noting that it was a "strange phrase."

92: infer. Confer, entrust, bestow.

105–106. For an excellent survey of the *topos,* the world as a stage, see Curtius, *European Literature,* pp. 138–44. Donne has warped the image for his own purpose: if men are actors, then they must be playing roles, and the best of them, the ones with the best parts, reenact her.

THE HARBINGER TO THE PROGRES

Title. Davenport cites E. F. Cheyney, *A History of England*, I, 54:

Among the prominent court officials was a knight harbinger, four ordinary harbingers and thirty yeomen of the crown who acted as messengers. It was the duty of these officials to go ahead to the place where the court was to be established, and secure in the vicinity of the palace lodgings for all court servants and officials who could not be accommodated in the Queen's own house there.

6: *The worlds last day, thy glories full degree.* The resurrection, when even bodies will become celestial, incapable of further change. Cf. lines 491–94 below.

7–8: *Still moued.* A paradoxical image of stasis in motion. In Ptolemaic astronomy the eighth sphere, the *Coelum Stellatum*, contained all the stars embedded in it, and although the sphere constantly revolved about the earth, carrying the stars with it, the stars themselves never moved.

9–10: *lugage.* Extremely heavy baggage that actually had to be lugged about on the back. *Clogged* is probably an allusion to the clay the body is made of. The implication is that the mud we are stuck in is what we carry about on our backs, our luggage, that is, ourselves.

16: *Iournals.* Either the events of your daily life or your journeys day by day, both of which amount to the same thing in this case.

23: *raught.* The past participle of reach, commonly used in the early seventeenth century.

27: mak'st her soules Hy progresse knowne. Davenport arrived at the correct reading by emendation, independent of the 1612 errata slip. Roger Bennett fared somewhat worse; he offered the emendation "mak'st her soul's by-progress known." I do not know what a by-progress is.

39–40. The reason for doubt is that the problem was never solved with any certainty. Augustine, for example, did not believe that the dead knew what was done on earth (*PL* 40, 604; see also 605, 607). Gregory, on the other hand, took the opposite point of view:

> Mortui, vita in carne viventium post eos qualiter disponatur, nesciunt; quia vita spiritus longe est a vita carnis. Quod tamen de animabus sanctis sentiendum non est; quia quae intus omnipotentis Dei claritatem vident, nullo modo credendum, quod sit foris aliquid quod ignorent. (*PL* 75, 999)

Aquinas attempted a half-hearted compromise:

> Respondeo dicendum quod secundum naturalem cognitionem, de qua nunc his agitur, animae mortuorum nesciunt quae hic aguntur. . . . Animae autem mortuorum secundum ordinationem divinam et secundum modum essendi segregatae sunt a conversatione viventium, et conjunctae conversationi spiritualium substantiarum quae sunt a corpore separatae; unde ea quae apud nos aguntur, ignorant.

But in the end he finally agreed with Gregory: "Magis tamen videtur, secundum sententiam Gregorii, quod animae sanctorum Deum videntes, omnia praesentia, quae hic aguntur, cognoscant. Sunt enim Angelis aequales" (*Summa,* I, Q. 89, a. 8).

THE SECOND ANNIVERSARY

1–6. The irony is complex. Donne first sardonically concedes only what proves his own point: since everything is still going on in darkness a year after it died, it must be, as his opponents say, somewhat eternal. But by granting them that he has forced them into an even more untenable position, for no one in the Renaissance believed that the world was eternal. The question was regarded as settled long before:

> De mundi . . . duratione locuti Aristot., Averroës, Cicero, Xenophanes illum aeternum, omnis corruptionis expertem dicunt. Nam cum non possent intelligere (ut Censorianus ait) ovane an aves ante generatae sunt, cum & ovum sine ave, & avis sine ovo gigni non posset: hinc arbitrari sunt mundum hunc, & uniuscujusque geniti initium simul & finem perpetua revolutione sempiternum. (Henricus Cornelius Agrippa ab Nettesheym, *De Incertitudine & Vanitate Omnium Scientiarum & Artium* [Lugduni Batavorum, 1643], p. 106)

See also Philo Judaeus, *De Aeternitate Mundi*, vii–xii; Guido Pancirolli, *Rerum Memorabilium . . . Commentarijs Illustrata . . . ab Henrico Salmuth* (Francofurti, 1660), II, 3; John Swan, *Speculum Mundi* (Cambridge, 1643), p. 1.

22: For there is motion in corruption. With perhaps the additional implication of maggots.

23–24. According to Genesis the sun and the stars were not created until the fourth day. There was considerable argument among exegetes over how there could be days when there was no sun. Nothing was settled, and Donne availed himself of the uncertainty to carry over some of the mystery into these lines. William Estius gives a fairly good survey of the controversy, citing the opinions of Augustine, Basil, and Aquinas (*Annotationes Aureae* [Coloniae Agrippinae, 1622], p. 2).

27–32. A new Deluge of forgetfulness, a Flood of Lethe. Cf.

> if it [sin] be above our head, then the brain is drown'd, that is, our reason, and *understanding*, which should dispute against it, and make us asham'd of it, or afraid of it; And our *memory* is drown'd, we

have forgot that there belongs a repentance to our sins, perchance forgot that there is such a sin in us; forgot that those actions are sins, forgot that we have done those actions; and forgot that there is a law, even in our own hearts, by which we might try, whether our actions were sins, or no. (*Sermons*, II, 110)

30: generall.   Universal, not just a regional problem. The most heated argument over the universality of the Deluge did not begin until the mid-seventeenth century with Isaac de la Peyrere and Isaac Vossius, but it had been touched upon earlier by the Church Fathers, who argued that Noah's Flood was not just a Jewish version of Deucalion's (D. C. Allen, *The Legend of Noah* [Urbana, Ill., 1949], pp. 74–75, 86–112).

33–36.   The songs are produced from the womb of Donne's mind, his female muse, which she inseminates. Cf. *Richard II*, V, v, 6–8:

> My brain I'll prove the female to my soul,
> My soul the father, and these two beget
> A generation of still breeding thoughts.

37: These Hymes.   A pun; the hymns are also males, which may impregnate others. Cf.

childrens children, are the Crown of the Elders, says *Solomon*: If when we have begot you in Christ, by our preaching, you also beget others by your holy life and conversation, you have added another generation unto us, and you have preached over our Sermons again, as fruitfully as we our selves; you shall be our Crown, and they shall be your Crowns, and Christ Jesus a Crown of everlasting glory to us all. (*Sermons*, III, 347)

42: Vntill man doe but vanish, and not die.

Taking then this Text for a probleme, *Quis homo, What man lives, and shall not see Death?* we answer, It may be those Men, whom

Christ shal find upon the earth alive, at his returne to Judge the
World, shall dye then, and it may be they shall but be changed, and
not dye. . . . Saint *Paul* sayes, *Behold I shew you a mystery;* Therefore it is not a cleare case, and presently, and peremptorily determined; but what is it? *We shall not all sleep, but we shall all be
changed.* But whether this sleeping be spoke of death itself, and exclude that, that we shall not die, or whether this sleep be spoke of
a rest in the grave, and exclude that, we shall not be buried, and
remain in death, that may be a mystery still. (*Sermons*, II, 204–205)

This was an important theological crux to Donne; he preached
an entire sermon on the subject and turned to it constantly
throughout his works. Cf. *Sermons*, VI, 67–88; I, 232; II, 70,
82, 210.

46: safe-sealing Bowle.   Grierson noted that *safe-sealing* was to
be found in the 1612 edition, but his collation was incorrect.
The text clearly reads *safe-fealing.* Nevertheless, I believe that
sealing is correct, even though the texts that print it have no
authority and it is not listed in the errata. Throughout his sermons Donne constantly refers to sacraments as seals ("a sacra-
ment is strictly taken to be a seal of grace," *Sermons*, II, 255).
Moreover, since it is used in relation to the Last Judgment, *sealing* probably refers to the seal which, according to the Apocalypse
7:3–4, will seal the servants of God "in their foreheads."

48: Hydropique.   Insatiably thirsty like a person diseased with
dropsy.

53: to try truths forth.   Test them to the end, thoroughly.

57–60.   Worms were traditionally known for their obliviousness
and insensitivity:

Nullum Vermibus ingenium, nulla memoria, nam Apibus Vespis
Crabronibusq́; hae dotes sunt. Quamobrem apud Lucianum merca-
tori, dum philosophum Scepticum Pyrrhiam interrogat an surdus

simul, & cęcus esset, respondet Pyrrhias, sensu se etiam & iudicio carere, breuiterq̃; nihil à Verme differre. Vnde est quòd quidam Vermes obliuiosas esse dixerint. (Ulysses Aldrovandus, *De Animalibus Insectis* [Bononiae, 1602], p. 641)

See also Ludovicus Caelius Rhodiginus, *Lectionum Antiquarum Libri Triginta* (Coloniae Allobrogum, 1620), p. 1105. Cf. lines 117–18 below.

66: congratulate. In the Latin sense of *congratulari,* to joy with. But see also *The First Anniversary,* line 2.

72: forme. In the Aristotelian-Scholastic sense of soul, that which gives life, movement, and individuality to a body. Cf. Aquinas, *Summa,* I, Q. 76, a. 1; Q. 110, a. 1.

75: tried. Purified by fire, refined, smelted. The metaphor is of a two-stage process removing the dross from metals.

78–80. Cf. "We say that the *Firmament* is full of *starres,* as though it were equally full; but we know, that there are more *stars* under the *Northerne,* then under the *Southern Pole*" (*Devotions,* p. 74). The information, however, was no longer regarded as scientifically correct:

> Si de stellis olim cognitis loquamur, septentrio longè plures numerat stellas quàm meridies. Verùm si consideremus sidera superiori seculo ab Indiae perlustratoribus obseruata, meridies plura numerat astra quam septentrio. Quod igitur quidam scribunt, Deum pluribus stellis haemisphaerium septentrionale tanquam nobilius exornasse, cum grano salis est accipiendum. (Alsted, II, 406)

82: rubbidge. A variant form of rubbish.

85–89. Donne apparently never made up his mind whether at death souls go to heaven or heaven comes to souls. In these lines it is presented one way; in lines 185–205 below it is the other; and a similar confusion is found in the sermons:

Little know we, how little a way a soule hath to goe to heaven, when it departs from the body; Whether it must passe locally, through Moone, and Sun, and Firmament, (and if all that must be done, all that may be done, in lesse time then I have proposed the doubt in) or whether that soule finde new light in the same roome, and be not carried into any other, but that the glory of heaven be diffused over all, I know not, I dispute not, I inquire not. (VII, 383; see also VIII, 175)

92: *Diuision.* Both a run or rapid melodic passage in music, considered as the division of a few long notes into a number of short ones, and death itself, the division of body and soul.

102–106. The irony is intricate pivoting on the word *Legacies.* *Sergeants* refers specifically to law officers. The devils are about to arrest the soul for debt (*OED*, sb. 4); they are not there for legacies in the usual sense of the word. But, says Donne, think the opposite of what is happening. Give them bequests. Will them all your sins, and after you are through, trust God to pay off whatever you still owe.

117. *Insensibly* is ambiguous, referring both to the maggots and the dead body.

120: saint Lucies night. December 13, according to the Julian calendar, the longest night in the year.

123: Complexion. The particular combination of her four humors. If, as Donne says, these were completely balanced in her, she was in perfect health when she died ("Sanitas est harmonia quatuor humorem," Alsted, II, 127). But she was also a miracle: "For a Body so equally tempered, so evenly ballanced by the Elements, that there should be no *praedominancie,* no struggling or wrestling in it, may be imagined; but surely (I thinke) was never really subsisting in Nature, nor well can be" (Hakewill, *An Apologie,* p. 31). All sublunary compounds were thought to be inevitably subject to dissolution simply because of their constituent contrariety: "Non . . . invenitur corruptio, nisi ubi invenitur contrarietas; generationes enim et corruptiones ex contrariis in contraria sunt. Unde corpora caelestia, quia non habent materiam contrarietati subjectam, incorruptibilia sunt" (Aquinas, *Summa*, I, Q. 75, a. 6; see also Plato, *Phaedo*, 78c; Cicero, *Tusc. Disp.*, I, xxix, 71; Alsted, II, 119–20).

125: no Feare, no Art could guesse. The image is extremely compressed, but its underlying form is clear enough if seen from a distance. Donne has just completed a meditation on the process of ordinary death (lines 85–120). Consequently, in this section, the eulogy, he contrasts it with the miracle of her deathbed. She was dying, but no one could tell how, even though her loved ones looked with the anxiety of fear and her physicians with the professional awareness of their art.

127: Mithridate. One of the most famous of all antidotes against poison, supposedly discovered by Mithridates VI, King of Pontus (120?–63 B.C.). Like *just* (exactly measured and blended) *perfumes*, it was composed of innumerable ingredients. For the full prescription, see Celsus, *De Medicina*, V, xxiii, 3. Pliny, however, mentions two others. One is composed of fifty-four ingredients (*Nat. Hist.*, XXIX, 8); the other was reportedly discovered among Mithridates' secret papers after his defeat by Pompey the Great (XXIII, 77).

131–134. Cf. "Subiectum Geometriae est magnitudo, id est, quantitas continua . . . : ita vt linea nihil sit aliud, quàm punctum continuè productum. Ita superficies est linea continuata: & corpus est continuata superficies" (Alsted, II, 298; see also *The Elements of the Most Ancient Philosopher Euclide of Megara*, trans. H. Billingsly [London, 1570], fols. 1a–2a). *Quantities* refers to geometrical figures in general, limited here contextually to those of at least two dimensions.

137–138. The sun, like all superlunary bodies, was believed to be composed of celestial matter not subject to contrariety and therefore neither to disease nor dissolution. Cf. Aquinas, *Summa*, I, Q. 75, a. 6, quoted in the notes to line 123 above; see also Marcus Antonius Natta, *Opera* (Venetiis, 1564), p. 12.

137: wonne. Overcome its unwillingness, prevail upon, induce.

138: venter. A variant form of venture.

139–140. Spirits (such as souls, angels, and devils) were thought to be simple, non-compounded beings. They could never be divided because there was nothing to separate:

> dubitare non possumus . . . quin nihil sit animis admixtum, nihil copulatum, nihil coagamentatum, nihil duplex. Quod cum ita sit, certe nec secerni nec dividi nec discerpi nec distrahi potest, ne interire quidem igitur. Est enim interitus quasi discessus et secretio ac diremptus earum partium, quae ante interitum coniunctione aliqua tenebantur. (Cicero, *Tusc. Disp.*, I, xxix, 71)

See also Plato, *Phaedo*, 78; Aquinas, *Summa*, I, Q. 75, a. 6; C. F. d'Abra de Raconis, *Tractatus de anima rationali* (Parisiis, 1632), pp. 350–91.

143–146. The so-called "aurea catena Homeri" (*Iliad*, VIII, 19), variously allegorized. Plato first identified it as the sun (because "so long as the sun and the heavens go round in their orbits, all things human and divine are and are preserved," *Theaetetus*, 153). In the Renaissance it was regarded by Neoplatonists as the inexorable concatenation of natural cause and effect: "Quid ergo Platoni fiet, qui ex Homeri sententia auream catenam fingit a Jove demitti coelitus, nisi causarum naturalium seriem inviolabilem ac plane immutabilem demus?" (Jean Bodin, *Colloquium Heptaplomeres*, ed. Ludovicus Noach [Suerini Megaloburgiensium, 1857], p. 23; see also Jonathan Swift, *The Battle of the Books* in *The Prose Works*, ed. Temple Scott [London, 1919], I, 174–75; for an excellent survey of the range of interpretations, see Franciscus Floridus Sabinus, *Lectionum Subcisiuarum* in *Lampas, sive Fax Artium Liberallum,* ed. Ianus Gruterus [Francofurti, 1602], I, 1156–59; for further bibliography, see Curtius, *European Literature,* p. 110*n*).

146: Accident. A complex pun meaning both chance, occurrence, mishap, and any event or occurrence. Since this is the chain of fate, its inviolable accidents (*events*) can never be accidents (*mishaps*). Beyond that, the word is also used in the philosophical sense of *accidens.*

147: meat. Food in general.

149–156. The underlying metaphor presents an action of disseizin:

> *Disseisin* (*Disseisina*) commeth of the French (*Disseisir*) and signifieth in the Common Lawe, an vnlawfull dispossessing of a man of his land, tenement or other immoveable or incorporeall right. . . . Disseisin is of two sorts; either simple disseisin, committed by day without force and armes . . . And Disseisin by force, (Cowell, *The Interpreter, s.v. Disseisin*)

The entire case is ironic, however, since this good man paradoxically pleads the exact points that should render such an action unnecessary. He has title, the strength to have assumed the title, and long possession. Nevertheless the property is not actually his until he wins the suit against himself. His own life disseizes him.

151–152. Matthew 11:12: "And from the days of John the Baptist until now the kingdom of heaven suffereth violence, and the violent take it by force." Cf. "from the time of *John Baptist,* the *kingdome of heaven suffers violence,* and every *violent* Man, that is, every earnest, and zealous, and spiritually valiant Man, may take hold of it" (*Sermons,* II, 220).

151: pretend. To put forward, offer for consideration, present as evidence.

158: sinke. A cesspool or sewer. As transferred to the body, it was the stomach, full of excrement. Donne's attitude toward the creation of the soul in this section is curiously ambivalent, veering from what seems to be creation *ex traduce* in lines 157–58 to creation *ex nihilo* in lines 159–68. Apparently he had not yet made up his mind which he believed. In a letter to Sir Thomas Lucy dated 8 October 1607, he admitted that in both opinions "there appear such infirmities as it is time to look for a better." If one follows the first, he can never prove that the soul is immortal or that mankind has any more than one soul; if, on the other hand, he chooses the second, he can never defend the doctrine of original sin, unless he is willing to admit that God forces souls to assume it (Gosse, *Life and Letters,* I, 175–76). Eventually, Donne took a stand on creation *ex nihilo,* but it was only after his ordination. Cf. *Sermons,* I, 177; II, 58–59, 85, 358; III, 109.

159–162. The doctrine of the threefold soul of man was a commonplace as old as Aristotle's *De Anima;* cf. Aquinas, *Summa,* I, Q. 76, a. 3, and Burton, I, i, 2, 5–9. Donne himself, however, supplies the best gloss:

> First, in a naturall man wee conceive there is a soule of vegetation and of growth; and secondly, a soule of motion and of sense; and then thirdly, a soule of reason and understanding, an immortall soule. And the two first soules of vegetation, and of sense, wee conceive to arise out of the temperament, and good disposition of the substance of which that man is made, they arise out of man himselfe; But the last soule, the perfect and immortall soule, that is immediately infused by God. (*Sermons,* III, 85)

In another sermon Donne explains that "at our inanimation in our Mothers womb, our immortall soule when it comes, swallowes up the other soules of vegetation, and of sense, which were in us before" (II, 358). Donne apparently thought that it devoured them like a cannibal in order to assimilate them literally into itself.

163: obnoxious. An uncommon use of the root meaning of the word: frail, infirm, exposed or liable to harm. Besides this of Donne's, the *OED* cites only one other example.

164–168. This seems straightforward enough, but Donne may mean that original sin is derived not from the body alone, but from its union with the soul, a position he held consistently throughout his sermons:

> In the generation of *our parents,* we were *conceiv'd in sin;* that is, they sinn'd in that action; so we were conceiv'd in sinne; in *their sin.* And in *our selves,* we were submitted to sin, in that very act of generation, because then we became in part the subject of *Originall sin.* Yet, there was no arrow shot *into* us then; there was no sinne in that *substance* of which we were made; for if there had been sin in that *substance,* that substance might be damn'd, though God should never infuse a soul into it; . . . and here's no arrow shot neither; here's no sin in *that* soul, that God creates. . . . Here's no arrow shot from the body, no sin in the *body alone;* None from the soul, no sin in the *soul alone;* And yet, the *union* of this soul and body is so accompanied with Gods *malediction* for our first transgression, that in the instant of that *union* of life, as certainly as that *body must die,* so certainly *the whole Man* must be guilty of *Originall sin.* (*Sermons,* II, 58–59; see also I, 177; III, 109)

165: This curded milke. Cf. Job 10: 9–10: "Remember, I beseech thee, that thou hast made me as the clay; and wilt thou bring me into dust again? Hast thou not poured me out as milk, and curdled me like cheese?"

169–172. Cf.

> L'enfant estant au ventre de sa mere, commence a vriner soudain que toutes ses parties sont formées, par le conduit de l'Vmbilic nommé *Vrachus,* mais aux derniers mois, prochains de sa natiuité, ledit *Vrachus* se ferme, comme auons dit, & alors l'enfant masle vrine par la verge, la femelle par le col de la vessie. Cette vrine se conserve auec

les autres excremens, à scauoir, la sueur, & les serositez, & autres superfluitez du sang menstruel, qui seruent pour supporter plus facilement l'enfant nageant en icelles: & lors que le temps est venu d'enfanter, il rompt les membranes, & adonc lesdites aquositez sortent, & lors les matrones predisent que bien tost la femme accouchera, puis que les eaux s'ecoulent. (Paré, *Oeuvres*, p. 595)

For a much longer, more detailed, and perhaps more scientific account, see Hieronymus Fabricius, *De Formato Foetu* (Venetiis, 1600), pp. 128–38.

184–218. By the end of this section (lines 214–18), Donne's customary ambivalence about the state of the soul immediately after death has almost worked itself around to the exact opposite of what he begins with, although he may have had the full implications of the ambiguity in mind to begin with, as here:

my soule, as soone as it is out of my body, is in Heaven, and does not stay for the possession of Heaven, nor for the fruition of the sight of God, till it be ascended through ayre, and fire, and Moone, and Sun, and Planets, and Firmament, to that place which we conceive to be Heaven, but without the thousanth part of a minutes stop, as soone as it issues, is in a glorious light, which is Heaven, (for all the way to Heaven is Heaven; And as those Angels, which came from Heaven hither, bring Heaven with them, and are in Heaven here, So that soule that goes to Heaven, meets Heaven here; and as those Angels doe not devest Heaven by comming, so these soules invest Heaven, in their going.) . . . my soule shall not goe towards Heaven, but goe by Heaven to Heaven, to the Heaven of Heavens. (*Sermons*, VII, 71)

See also the notes to lines 85–89 above.

195: trie. Discover, know.

197–200. I. A. Shapiro noted (*TLS*, 3 July, 1937) that Donne apparently adopted Tycho Brahe's planetary sequence in this section since he placed Venus before Mercury and not in reversed order, as they are in the normal Ptolemaic arrangement. The point of the passage, however, is that such things do not matter.

197–198.   Cf. Donne's "Problem 9": *"Why is Venus-star multinominous, called* Hesperus *and* Vesper" (*Paradoxes and Problems,* pp. 54–55).

199.   Cf. Ovid, *Meta.,* I, 622–723.

200: who now is growen all Ey.   As long as souls are immured in bodies, they perceive only through the organs of sense, but as soon as they become free they are able to perceive directly through themselves in all directions at once, as though every part of them were eye. Cf. Dryden's imitation of the line:

> O happy soul! if thou canst view from high
> Where thou art all intelligence, all eye.
>   (*Eleonora,* 340–41)

214–215.   Cf.

> There are in this man, this Christian, *Tres nativitates,* sayes S. *Gregory,* three births; one, *Per generationem,* so we are borne of our naturall mother; one *Per regenerationem,* so we are borne of our spirituall Mother, the Church, by Baptisme; and a third, *Per Resurrectionem,* and so we are borne of the generall Mother of us all, when the earth shall be delivered, not of twins, but of millions . . . in the Resurrection. (*Sermons,* VI, 134–35)

In the verse Donne probably made a change in the third birth for theological reasons. Unlike many Fathers of the Church and a number of Protestants of his time, he did not believe that the Beatific Vision was denied man until after the general Resurrection. Instead, he agreed with the Catholic position, that immediately after death the souls of the just find themselves in heaven —precisely what he has been demonstrating in this entire section.

For an excellent essay on the topic, see Helen Gardner's "Appendix A," in her edition of the *Divine Poems* (Oxford, 1952), pp. 114–17.

219: long-short Progresse. Long in space, short in time.

224: others beauties. *Others* is by far the better reading. It doubles the sense of fragmentation: not that they are beauties in themselves, but that each has only a small part of the beauty she possessed.

226: prefer. Promote, elevate for the purposes of comparison.

235–240. In other works Donne uses the idea explicitly to satirize Roman Catholics. Cf.

> if he [the Pope] would come to a true and reall exercise of all that power which they attribute to him, I doubt not, but that Angell, which hath so long serued in the place of being the particular *Assistant* in the *Conclaue*, (for, since they affoord a particular *Tutelar Angell* to euerie *Colledge* and *Corporation*, And *to the race of Flyes and of Fleas, and of Ants,* since they allowe such an *Angell* to *euery Infidell Kingdome, yea to Antichrist, yea to Hell it selfe,* it were verie vnequall to denie one to this place,) This *Angell,* I say, would be glad of the roome, and become a Suiter to the *holy Ghost,* to name him in the next *Conclaue.* (*Pseudo-Martyr,* pp. 248–49)

See also Gosse, *Life and Letters,* II, 8. According to the marginal reference, Donne got the information from Andreas Victorellus' *De Angelorum Custodia* (1605). Victorellus offers a remarkable example of the precise sort of thing Donne is laughing at:

> Non solamente gli Imperii, i Regni, le Prouincie, le Nationi: ma le Diocesi, le Città, le Castella, le Fortezze, le Ville, le Parochie: & singolarmente le Congregationi Religio se tutte, le parti loro, cioè le Prouincie prima, & poi i Monasterij sono in tutela di Angeli particolari, i Collegij de' Sacerdoti secolari ancora, i Seminarij de'

Cherici, le Congregationi, le Famiglie medesime di persone secolari sono state da Dio date in guardia a proprij, & destinti gouernatori della sua Corte. Aggiungete i Capitani di efferciti di buon Prencipe (maggiori, & minori) gli efferciti stessi, & le loro parti, (in giusto guerre però) le naui, le galee, per giusta difesa, o per giusti acquisti alla inconstanza del mar esposte. (*Trattato della Custodia, c'hanno i Beati Angeli de gli huomini* [Venetia, 1610], pp. 39–40)

241–243. Cf.

Omni auro inest argentum vario pondere, alibi nona, alibi octava parte. . . . Ubicumque quinta argenti portio est, electrum vocatur. . . . Et electro auctoritas, Homero teste qui Menelai regium auro, electro argento, ebore fulgere tradit. Minervae templum habet Lindos, insulae Rhodiorum, in quo Helena sacravit calycem ex electro. Adjicit historia, mammae suae mensura. (Pliny, *Nat. Hist.*, XXXIII, 23)

See also Pliny, IX, 40; *Sermons*, III, 300.

245: wrought. Worked.

259–260. There were a great number of treatises on the immortality of the soul in the early days of the Renaissance, all proclaiming definite proof and all contradicting each other. By Donne's time an inevitable reaction had set in, and most learned men agreed with Petrus Pomponatus (the so-called atheist) that it was an article of faith, not reason:

omnis ars debet per propria & convenientia arti procedere, aliter peccat & inartificiose procedit . . . : sed animam esse immortalem est articulus fidei, ut patet per symbolum Apostolarum & Athanasii: Ergo probari debet per propria fidei, medium autem quo innititur fides est revelatio & Scriptura Canonica: tantum vere & proprie per haec habet probari: Caetera vero rationes sunt extraneae, innituntur quo medio non probante quod intenditur: non igitur mirum est si philosophi inter se discordant de immortalitate animae, cum argumentis extraneis conclusioni, & fallacibus innituntur: At omnes

Christicolae concordes cum per propria & infallibilia procedunt, cum haec non possint esse nisi secundum unum modum. (*De Immortalitate Animae* [Lugduni Batavorum, 1534], pp. 144–45)

See also John Woolton, *A treatise of the immortalite of the soule* (London, 1576), fols. 2b, 67a; Jacob Calerus, *De animae immortalitate* (Witebergae, 1587), fol. 2a.

266: new ingredients. Salt, sulphur, and mercury according to Paracelsus and his disciples. Cf.

> when *Galen* mentions in his time but three sects of Physitians, *Emperikes, Methodists* and *Dogmatiques;* we haue now a fourth that goe vnder the name of *Chymiques, Hermetiques,* or *Paracelsians,* & a branch of them (as I conceiue, is the order *Roseae Crusis*) who treading in the steppes of their *master,* haue changed Aristotles 3 principles of naturall bodies, *matter, forme,* and *priuation;* into Salt, Sulphur, and Mercury; and from the seuerall temper of these three, they affirme all sicknesses and health to arise. (Hakewill, *An Apologie,* pp. 244–45)

For a much more extended, detailed account, see Alsted, IV, 418.

269–278. The stones in the bladder and mucus in the lungs are simply examples of medical problems. No particular controversy about them is known. The movement of blood from one ventricle to the other, however, was debated by all the authorities—Vesalius, Columbus, Botallus, Paré. Nails and hair were also a mystery. Authorities were uncertain whether they were actually parts of the body and, if so, whether they were skin, organs, bones or excrement (Allen, "Renaissance Medicine," pp. 331, 333, 338*n*).

290: In this low forme. A pun on classes in the English school system. Heaven contains the upper forms (lines 301–302) and earth the lower.

292: Fantasy. In scholastic psychology the part of the mind that receives the impressions from the various senses and synthesizes them, presenting to the intellect an image of the thing perceived (cf. Ioannes di Napoli, *Manuale Philosophiae* [Romae, 1951], III, 489–90). As long as souls are joined to bodies, they are incapable of perceiving universals without first abstracting them from the supply of images presented by the phantasy. As soon as they become free, however, they perceive ideas directly, as they are in essence. Cf. Aquinas, *Summa,* I, Q. 84, a. 7:

> Utrum intellectus possit actu intelligere per species intelligibiles quas penes se habet, non convertendo se ad phantasmata. . . . Respondeo dicendum, quod impossibile est intellectum nostrum secundum praesentis vitae statum quo passibili corpori conjungitur, aliquid intelligere in actu, nisi convertendo se ad phantasmata . . . ; quando aliquis conatur aliquid intelligere, format sibi aliquid phantasmata per modum exemplorum, in quibus quasi inspiciat quod intelligere studet.

See also *Summa,* I, Q. 75, a. 6; Q. 85, a. 1; Q. 86, a. 1.

294: watch-towre. A traditional symbol of the mind. For an excellent survey of the *topos,* see D. C. Allen, *The Harmonious Vision: Studies in Milton's Poetry* (Baltimore, 1954), pp. 17–18, who cites Plato, *Timaeus,* 70a and the *Republic,* 560b; Isaiah 31: 5–8; Pliny, *Nat. Hist.,* XI, 134; Cicero, *De Nat. Deor.,* II, 140; and Spenser, *FQ,* II, ix, 44–58.

299–300. Cf.

> As he that fears God, fears nothing else, so, he that sees God, sees every thing else: when we shall see God, *Sicuti est,* as he is, we shall see all things *Sicuti sunt,* as they are; for that's their Essence, as they conduce to his glory. We shall be no more deluded with outward appearances: for, when this sight, which we intend here comes, there

will be no delusory thing to be seen. All that we have made as though we saw, in this world, will be vanished, and I shall see nothing but God, and what is in him. (*Sermons*, III, 111–12)

300. Shalt was commonly elided to *shall* before the consonant cluster *str.*

301–320. Donne's version of the traditional metaphor, the book of the mind: *liber rationis.* According to the usual formulation, the mind of man is a volume "qui est Dei aeterna ars et sapientia" because it contains within it an inscription of the divine ideas (Bonaventure, *Breviloquium*, II, 5 and John of Salisbury, *Policraticus*, I, 173, cited by Curtius, *European Literature*, pp. 320, 321). According to Donne, however, only she had wisdom and purity of mind enough to know universals in their essential form (lines 301–318). The rest of us perceived them best in her (lines 318–320) since we are capable of understanding them only as they exist in particulars. For the final book metaphor (line 320), Donne's variant of the well-known *liber mundi* or *liber creaturae*, see Curtius, pp. 319–26.

308: aie. Ever, always, continually; usually spelled *aye*, though *aie* or even *eie* were not uncommon. Cf. line 482 below. Other than in the *Anniversaries* Donne used the word only one other time in his poetry, in the sonnet "To Mr. C. B.," line 11: "Going to where sterne winter aye doth wonne." The emendation *all* is superficially convincing, but it has no authority. The 1625 edition corrupted *aie* to *are*, and since the 1633 edition was set directly from the 1625, the editor had no choice but to make a change.

316: ouer-fraite. Cause to sink from too much weight. Cf. "Air and Angels," line 18, and the note in Theodore Redpath's edition of the *Songs and Sonets* (London, 1956), p. 32.

331–332. Cf. "Beloved, . . . no things are liker one another, then *Court* and *Court,* the same ambitions, the same underminings in one Court as in another" (*Sermons,* III, 123).

333–334. Courts are so evil that even their libelers cannot keep up with them.

335–336. Cf.

> Scire . . . convenit non omnia venena cor primùm petere, & illi noxiam inferre. Siquidem reperiuntur, quibus ita natura comparatum est (id enim claret experientia) ut intus assumpta separatim noceant uno tantùm corporis membro alia verò alteri . . . ; planè constat cantharidas praecipuè noxam inferre vesciae cicutam cerebro, leporem marinum pulmoni, & alia item aliis corporis membris particularibus. (Pietro Andrea Mattioli, *Opera Omnia* [Basileae, 1674], p. 973)

See also Paré, *Oeuvres,* p. 482.

337: excrements. A pun of sorts; nails and hair were also regarded as excrement: "Inter excrementa pili quoq; cōnumerantur, & ungues" (Raphael Volaterranus, *Commentariorum Urbanarum* [Lugduni, 1552], p. 755). See also Thomas Nashe, *Works,* ed. R. B. McKerrow, rev. F. P. Wilson (Oxford, 1958), II, 227, 230; *Sermons,* VII, 177.

338: So will. This may be an instance of revision in the errata. The variant *So wise* (meaning in that way or manner) is possible, though it is not a common form. The *OED* offers only one late example: Tennant's *Papistry Storm'd* (1827), "Sae-wyse the Papists . . . Did scatter aff." In Donne's time, however, the use of *wise* compounds in general was much more common than it is today. Consequently it is possible that Donne first wrote *So wise,* reconsidered it when he drew up the errata slip, and made the correction, thinking that the compound might be too unfamiliar, as it was to the editor of the 1633 text, who rimed out the emendation *lyes.*

339–358. The order of the hierarchy loosely corresponds to the major headings in the first part of the *Litany of the Saints.* The *Litany* begins with Mary, the Angels and Archangels, Patriarchs and Prophets, Apostles, Martyrs, Doctors, Bishops, Confessors, Holy Virgins, Widows, and finally all Holy Men and Women. For an abbreviated version similar to Donne's, see Iacobus Merlo Horstius, *Paradisus Animae Christianae* (Coloniae Agrippinae, 1644), pp. 516–21; see also Donne's "Litanie," stanzas v–xiv.

341–342. Free of original sin. Cf.

> He came into the world; it is not *in mundam,* into so clean a woman as had no sin at all, none contracted from her Parents, no original sin; for so Christ had placed his favours and his honors ill, if he had favoured her most who had no need of him: to dye for all the world, and not for his mother, or to dye for her, when she needed not that hell, is a strange imagination: she was not without sin; for then why should she have died? for even a naturall death in all that come by natural generation, is of sin. (*Sermons,* I, 307)

343–344. Luke 11:27–28: "And it came to pass, as he spoke these things, a certain woman of the company lifted up her voice, and said unto him, Blessed is the womb that bore thee, and the paps which thou hast sucked. But he said, Yea rather, blessed are they that hear the word of God, and keep it."

351–352. A variant of the proverb "Semen ecclesiae sanguis est martyrum." Cf. "At what a high rate did the blessed Martyrs sell their bodies; They built up Gods Church with their blood: They sowed his field, and prepared his harvest with their blood" (*Sermons,* I, 157; see also I, 162; *Biathanatos,* p. 63).

360: royalties. Prerogatives; the rights, privileges, and duties of the head of state.

363–364. Cf. Psalm 85:10: "Mercy and truth are met together; righteousness and peace have kissed each other." The paradox of chaste beauty was a commonplace that had appealed to Donne before; cf. *"Why are the Fairest, Falsest," Paradoxes and Problems,* pp. 49–50.

371: protections.   Specifically, protections *cum clausula volumus:*

> Protection . . . is vsed for an exemption, or an immunity giuen by the King to a person against suites in law, or other vexations vpon reasonable causes him thereunto mouing, which I take to be a branch of his prerogatiue. And of this protection, *Fitzh.* maketh two sorts. . . . The first forme or sort he calleth a protection, *cum clausula volumus,* whereof he mentioneth foure particulars. A protection, *quia profecturus,* for him that is to passe ouer sea in the kings service: A protectiõ *quia moratur,* for him that is abroad in the Kings seruice vpon the sea, or in the marches. . . . A protection for the Kings debter, that he be not siewed or attached vntill the King be payed his debt. . . . And a protection in the Kings service beyond the seas, or on the marches of Scotland. The second forme of protection is termed *cû clausula, Nolumus:* which is graunted most commonly to a spirituall company for their immunity from taking of their catell by the Kings ministers. (Cowell, *The Interpreter, s.v. Protection*)

382: accidentall ioyes in Heauen doe grow.   The essential joy of heaven is the everlasting possession of the Beatific Vision; all others are its accidents. Cf.

> The blessednesse of heaven it selfe, Salvation, and the fruits of Paradise . . . have yet got no other name in the subtilty of the Schools, nor in the fulnesse of the Scriptures, but to be called the joys of heaven; Essentiall blessednesse is called so, *Enter into thy Masters joy,* that is, into the Kingdome of heaven; and accidentall happinesse added to that essentiall happinesse is called so too: There is joy in heaven at the conversion of a sinner; and so in the *Revelation, Rejoyce ye heavens, and yee that dwell in them, for the accuser of our brethren is cast down.* (Sermons, III, 339)

See also lines 440–44, 449–54, 467–70, and 487–96 below.

385–386. "The law of England is, that so long as the principall is not attainted, the accessorie may not be dealt with" (Cowell, *The Interpreter, s.v. Accessory*).

390: moue. To arouse with emotion, stir one's affections.

391: couse'ned cose'nor. Double-crossed double-crosser; lines 397–400 explain why.

401–405. Cf. "he [God] is content to receive his Honour from us, (for although all cause of Honour be eternally inherent in himselfe, yet that Act proceeds from us, and of that Honour, which is in *Honorante,* he could have none, til he had made Creatures to exhibit it)" (*Essays in Divinity,* p. 54).

406: But that, to his hands, man might grow more fit. That man might become more worthy of his creator through spiritual progress. It was traditionally assumed that Adam would have improved if he had not fallen:

> Posuit . . . Deus hominem in paradisum quasi in locum disciplinae et scholam virtutem, ut ibi per obedientiam mandati exercitaretur, accepturus si persisteret praemium, si praevaricaretur, poenam. Quapropter in paradiso solum bonum, sed non summum positum est, ut in eo quod solum erat bonum a puritate virtus inciperet, in eo autem quod summum non erat bonum esset quo exercitata proficeret. (Hugh of St. Victor, *PL* 176, 723)

See also Aquinas, *Summa,* I, Q. 102, a. 4; Pico della Mirandola, *De Hominis Dignitate,* ed. Eugenio Garin, *Edizione Nazionale* (Firenze, 1942), pp. 104, 106; Milton, *Paradise Lost,* V, 493–503; *Sermons,* II, 123; VII, 108.

417–422. Cf.

Men have considered usefully the incongruity of building the towre of Babel, in this, That to have erected a Towre that should have carried that height that they intended in that, the whole body of the earth, the whole Globe, and substance thereof would not have served for a basis, for a foundation to that Towre. If all the timber of all the forests in the world, all the quarries of stones, all the mines of Lead and Iron had beene laid together, nay if all the earth and sea had beene petrified, and made one stone, all would not have served for a basis, for a foundation of that Towre; from whence then must they have had their materials for all the superedifications? (*Sermons*, VIII, 322–23).

The source of the information is unknown. D. C. Allen noted that the ideas seem to have been original in some degree with Donne (*MLN*, LXIV [1949], 481–83). Later in the century, however, the same objections are found in Athanasius Kircher's *Turris Babel*, and it is highly unlikely that he derived them from Donne. After calculating the distance between the earth and the moon as 178,672 miles, Kircher estimated that a tower built from one to the other would occupy 374,354,625,000,000,000 cubic feet, an obvious impossibility:

Si omnium sylvarum totius orbis terrarum ligna in unum locum fuissent comportata, & totus orbis terrarum in limum, seu argillam cessisset, & oceanus cum omnibus maribus & fluviis in bitumen; nec ligna ad coquendos lateres, nec argillam orbem terrae, nec ad bitumen oceanum suffecturum fuisse. Novum igitur orbem condere, eumque hoc duplo majorem ad hanc fabricam expediendam esse oportebat.

Kircher concludes that the weight of the tower would force the earth away from the center of the universe and destroy the entire fabric of the world: "ergò totus terrenus globus extra centrum universi, cum ruina totius Mundi extisset" (Amstelodami, 1679, pp. 39–40).

425–428. Cicero mentions the worship of "Amor, Dolus, Morbus, Labor, Invidentia, Fatum, Senectus, Mors, Tenebrae, Miseria,

Querella, Gratia, Fraus, Pertinacia, Parcae, Hesperides, Somnia."
He also notes that "perniciosis . . . rebus non modo nomen
deorum tribueretur, sed etiam sacra constituerentur. Febris enim
fanum in Palatio et Orbonae ad aedum Larum et aram Malae
Fortunae Esquiliis consecratam videmus" (*De Deorum Natura*,
III, xvii, 44; xxv, 63). Iuvenal contributed the deified onion
(*Satira* XV, 9–11; see also Tertullian, *Ad Nationes, PL* 1, 600,
606; Hakewill, *An Apologie,* pp. 304–305; *Essays in Divinity,* p.
22; *Sermons,* III, 83; IX, 125).

435: pitch. Highest point, peak; also used as the height to
which a falcon or hawk rises before stooping to its prey.

439. Superficially the line seems straightforward enough: we
should think about heaven twice as much as we think about
earth. But Donne may also mean that we should take every
thought we have on earth and double it by extending it outward
both ways to its logical conclusion in the circumference, for God
is everywhere, the beginning and the end.

440: All will not serue. A difficult phrase. It implies the doctrine of election, but refers back specifically to thoughts. All our
thoughts, even doubled, would not be enough since the actual
perception of God is dependent on God to reveal it ("both the
obiect, and the wit").

440–442. Cf. Aquinas, *Summa,* I, Q. 12, a. 4:

> impossibile est quod aliquis intellectus creatus per sua naturalia
> essentiam Dei videat. . . . Relinquitur . . . quod cognoscere ipsum
> esse subsistens sit connaturale soli intellectui divino, et quod sit supra
> facultatem naturalem cujuslibet intellectus creati: quia nulla crea-
> tura est suum esse, sed habet esse participatum. Non igitur potest
> intellectus creatus Deum per essentiam videre, nisi in quantum Deus
> per suam gratiam se intellectui creato conjungit ut intelligibile ab
> ipso.

See also *Sermons*, VII, 254. For the background of Aquinas' discussion, see Aristotle, *Metaphysics*, 175a and Plotinus, *Ennead*, V, i, 7: that God, absolute unity, does not conceive by subject—object relationships, but contains the object by the act of apprehending it.

445–446. In the first instant of creation, the angels looked into themselves in amazement at existence. Then some of them looked up immediately to find the source of their being and saw the primordial essence of all things in the Word; others, however, fell in love with themselves and like Narcissus drowned in their own darkness. They never saw the face of God. Augustine began the tradition in his discussion of angelic cognition in *De Genesi ad Litteram*, IV, 22–35, but Aquinas codified it:

> instans primum in Angelis intelligitur respondere operationi mentis angelicae, qua se in se ipsam convertit per vespertinam cognitionem; quia in primo die commemoratur vespere, sed non mane. Et haec quidem operatio in omnibus bona fuit. Sed ab hac operatione quidam per matutinam cognitionem ad laudem Verbi sunt conversi; quidam vero in se ipsis remanentes facti sunt nox, per superbiam intumescentes, ut Augustinus dicit, 4 super Gen. ad litt., c. 24. Et sic primo operatio fuit omnibus communis; sed in secunda sunt distincti. Et ideo in primo instanti omnes fuerunt boni, sed in secundo fuerunt boni a malis distincti. (*Summa*, I, Q. 63, a. 6)

See also *Summa*, I, Q. 58, a. 6. For Donne's familiarity with the tradition, see *Sermons* III, 254; VIII, 105, 361; X, 180.

464: Who dreamt deuoutlier, then most vse to pray. Cf. "those Saints of God who have their Heaven upon earth, doe praise him in the night; according to that of S. *Ierome, Sanctis ipse somnus, oratio;* and that of S. *Basil, Etiam somnia Sanctorum preces sunt;* That holy men doe praise God, and pray to God in their sleep, and in their dreames" (*Sermons*, VIII, 53; see also II, 227; VIII, 202; X, 220). I was unable to find the passage in Jerome; Basil, however, writes:

neque patiare mediam vitae partem inutilem tibi esse per somni soporem: sed dividatur tibi noctis tempus in somnum et precationem: imo somnus ipse exercitatio sit pietatis. Saepe enim expressae in somno species nescio quomodo vestigia quaedam ac reliquiae esse solent diurnarum curarum. . . . Sic orabis *Sine ulla intermissione,* si modo non in verbis praecationem concludas, sed te ipse Deo conjunxeris per totam vivendi rationem; adeo ut jugis assiduaque precatio vita tua sit. (*PG* 31, 243, 246)

See also *PG* 32, 1239.

473: casuall. Non-essential, accidental in the philosophical sense, but also with a pun on the more ordinary meaning fortuitous, accidental, subject to chance.

477–481. Cf.

A Postume is gathered of superfluitie of humours in some member, and maketh rotting and swelling. . . . [It] commeth in this manner: While humeurs haue default in quantitie, and maye not be wasted by heat, nor put out by strẽgth of vertue, they be receiued in the hollowness of members, & ther boyle & putrifie, & as paast set in an ouen, & dryed by fire, receiueth a manner crusting in the utter side, under the which crust the paast is softe: so the humour gathered, by heat boyleth and maketh a manner crust aboue, under the which crust rotted humor is hidde, and swelleth: and such a swellying is called *Apostema.* (*Batman vppon Bartholome,* fol. 110b)

See also Paré, *Oeuvres,* pp. 161–206. Batman's crust is Donne's bag. For well-known catalogues of those who died ironically in the throes of joy or laughter, see Pliny, *Nat. Hist.,* VII, 54, 32; Aulus Gellius, *Noct. Att.,* III, 15; Montaigne, *Essais,* I, 2.

477: Redresse. Remedy, relief, assistance.

498–500. Any attempt to explain the extent of her goodness can only insult her. A lion among rabbits is not the best rabbit.

507–508. By making full perfection fuller, she adds to (*peeces*) a circle (a traditional symbol of perfection) while still paradoxically keeping it a circle.

511–512. Donne was in France with Sir Robert Drury from the end of November, 1611, to the middle of April, 1612. See Introduction.

514–515: what lawes of poetry admit. Invocations; in poetry, the muses and deities, in Catholicism, the saints.

527–528. The trumpet is a common figure of the prophet, blasted by inspiration. Cf. Ezekiel:

> Again the word of the Lord came unto me, saying, Son of man, speak to the children of thy people and say unto them, When I bring the sword upon a land, if the people of the land take a man of their coasts, and set him for their watchman: If when he seeth the sword come upon the land, he blow the trumpet, and warn the people; Then whosoever heareth the sound of the trumpet, and taketh not warning; if the sword come, and take him away, his blood shall be upon his own head. . . . But he that taketh warning shall deliver his soul. . . . So thou, O son of man, I have set thee a watchman unto the house of Israel; therefore thou shalt hear the word at my mouth, and warn them from me. (33:1–7)

See also *Sermons*, II, 167–70. Like the trumpet that will sound eternity, Donne has called all men to a general resurrection:

> as at the last resurrection, all that heare the sound of the Trumpet, shall rise in one instant, though they have passed thousands of years between their burialls, so doe all ye, who are now called, by a lower and infirmer voice [the preacher of the word, the watchman, *Tuba Domini*], rise together in this resurrection of grace. Let him that hath been buried *sixty* years, *forty* years, *twenty* years, in covetousness, in uncleannesse, in indevotion, rise now, now *this minute*, and then, as *Adam* that dyed *five thousand* before, shall be no sooner in

heaven, in his body, then you, so *Abel* that dyed *for God*, so long before you, shall be no better, that is, no fuller of the glory of heaven, then you that dye *in God*, when it shall be his pleasure to take you to him. (*Sermons*, III, 133)

Cf. "Grace is the soule of the soule, and the departing of grace, is the death, and the returning of grace is the resurrection of this sinfull soule" (*Sermons*, VI, 71–72).

Index

S

T

V